DELICIOUSLY YOURS

DELICIOUSLY YOURS

Mumtaz Rahimtoola

and

Mumtaz Currim

Inside illustrations by Walter Machado

JAICO PUBLISHING HOUSE
Mumbai ● Delhi ● Bangalore
Calcutta ● Hyderabad ● Chennai

© 1976 Mumtaz A. Currim, Mumtaz A. Rahimtoola

No part of this book may be reproduced or utilized in any form or by any means, electronic or mechanical including photocopying, recording or by any information storage and retrieval system, without permission in writing from the publishers.

First edition 1976
Published by
India Book House,
Mumbai.

DELICIOUSLY YOURS
ISBN 81-7224-055-4

First Jaico Impression : 1982
Fourth Jaico Impression : 1992
Fifth Jaico Impression : 1994
Sixth Jaico Impression : 1996
Seventh Jaico Impression : 2000

Published by:
Ashwin J. Shah
Jaico Publishing House
121, Mahatma Gandhi Road
Mumbai - 400 001.

Printed by:
R.N. Kothari
Sanman & Co.,
113, Shivshakti Ind. Estate,
Marol Naka, Andheri (East)
Mumbai - 400 059.

CONTENTS

DELICIOUSLY YOURS

Jalebi Caramel	3
Pineapple Halwa	3
Potato Halwa	4
Bread Halwa	5
Stuffed Apples	5
Paneer Delight	6
Lasan Kheema	7
Dry Gosht Masala	7
Bhuna Gosht	8

SIMPLY YOURS

Railway Mutton Curry	11
Bengali Fish Curry	11
Shrimp and Corn Bake	12
Mulligatawny Mutton	12
Kheema Masala Tukre	13
Potato and Corn Rolls	14
White Mutton Curry	14
Mutton Masala Slices	15
Special Purees	15
Mince Steaks	16

Dubalo Chaval	16
Khurdi—Kitchri	17
Kitchri	17
Kudal Palidu	18
White (Safed) Trotters	19
Kheema Kababs	19
Chikoli Chaval	20
Fish Salan (Red)	20
Fish Curry (Green)	21
Coconut Milk Stew	22
Moong Curry	22
White Pumpkin Dhal	23
Palak Gosht (Meat with Spinach)	24
Green Shurwa	24
Red Shurwa	25
Mutton and Vegetable Shurwa	26
Mutton Do Piaza	26
Ab Gosht (Green)	27
Ab Gosht (Red)	28
Sweet 'N' Sour Mutton	28
Curried Corn	29
Botee Gosht Salan	29
Pea Potato Masala	30
Hyderabadi Masala Gosht	31
Aloo Gosht	31
Cauliflower Gosht	32
Shabh	32
Kababi Gosht	33
Katay Masalay ka Gosht	34
Keema Karela	34
Murg Tamater	35
Bihari Grilled Meat	35
Onion Salad	36

Shalgum Mutter Vegetable	36
Yakhni Pulao	37
Dhal Gosht	38
Konkani Salan	39
Pineapple Curry	39
Phalli Besan	40
Roti Salan	40
Lucknowi Tamatar Gosht	41
Meat in Tandur Roti	42

SPICILY YOURS

Lucknowi Bhuna Gosht	45
Zanzibar Fish Curry	45
Tomato Egg Curry	46
Pasande Kababs	47
Kakowri-ke-Kababs	47
Dahi Meat	48
Punjabi Chole	49
Dahi Chops	49
Pasande	50
Seekh Curry	51
Shami Kababs	51
Kaddul Channa	52
Baide-ki-Roti	52
Baingan Masala	53
Suki Dhal	54
Naan Chaap	54
Apple Chutney	55
Shredded Chicken Vindaloo	55
Kolmi Sirka Achar	56

Machali-Achar Punjabi	56
Pomfret Pickle	57
Kolmi Nariel Pulao	58
Prawn Pattia	58
Goan Masala Pomfret	59
Hara Masala Aloo	60
Lal Masala Aloo	60
Moong Ragda	61
Liver Masala	61
Raw Mango Preserve	62
Tomato Chutney	63
Sabzi Achar	63
Kidneys on Toast	64
Kidneys and Chops Masala	64
Masala Baked Pomfret	65
Fish Masala Rolls	65
Masala Spaghetti	66
Channa Batata	67
Dahi Batata	67
Sev Chaat	68
Aloo Chollas	68
Kohlapuri Gurde	69
Guava Chhat	70
Moghlai Dahi Aloo	70

ELABORATELY YOURS

Khowsway	73
Lagania Sheekh	74
Masala Jinga Pulao	74
Kitchra	75
Moothiyas	76

Kaju Chicken	77
Pulao in Layers	77
Kashmiri Gosht	78
Mutton Kohani	79
Mutton and Corn Pulao	79
Chicken Curry	80
Narg'si Kofta Korma	80
Mughlai Murgh Masala	81
Ajmeri Curry	82
Pulao Peshawari	83
Korma Shahi	83
Kababs Moghlai	84
Spinach Mutton Pulao	85
Baked Coconut Fish	86
Jaliwalla Cutlets	86
Harisa	87
Jali Chicken	88
Biryani	88
Moghlai Meat Roast	89
Prawn Biryani	90
Zaffrani Korma	91
Murgh Mussalam	91
Pasande Peshawari	92
Murgh Jehangiri	93
Moghlai Pulao Nurjehani	94
Moghlai Pulao Nargisi	95
Paayas	95
Jungbari Pulao	96
Masoor Pulao	97
Prawn Patia Rice Ring	98
Cheese Kofta Curry	99
Prawn Korma	100
Aakhi Murgi	100

Spinach Prawn Souffle	101
Meat in Bread Loaf	102
Murg and Makai Souffle	102
Walnut Meat Loaf	103
Ananas Salad	103
Spanish Chicken Rice	104

SWEETLY YOURS

Kaju Toffee	107
Zarda Pulao	107
Baide-ka-Halwa	108
Rice Cake	109
Fruit and Mava Ghas ka Halwa	109
Saffron Pista Cake	110
Freezer Strawberry Ice Cream	110
Mango Mousse	111
Chickoo Souffle	111
Sheer Khurma	112
Kaju Curd Delight	112
Kharbuz Gulab	112
Shahi Tukre	113
Mava Bread Bake	114
Doodhi-ka-Halwa	114
Roat	115
Caramel Phirni	116
Khopra Paak	116
Mah Khudi	117
Doodhi-ki-Mithas	117
Kele-ki-Kheer	118
Sweet Coconut Croquettes	118
Shahi Firni	119

Guava Custard	119
Mava Kesar Halwa	120
Mango Creme	120
Caramel Souffle	121
Choco-Nut Custard	121
Choc Semolina Whip	122
Gooseberry Mould	122
Strawberry Souffle	123
Pineapple Souffle	124
Banana Cloud	124
Strawberry Creme Tart	125
Chocolate Pear Trifle	126
Mock Cream	126
Lemon Fluff	127
Pineapple Delight	127
Malpuras	128

HELPFULLY YOURS

Equivalent Measures and Weights	131
Metric Equivalents	131
Oven Temperatures and Regulo Numbers	132
On Frying Well	132
On Frying Ground Spices (Masalas)	132
To Prevent Lumps	133
For Easy Grinding	133
Grated Onions	134
To Skin Tomatoes	134
On Boiling Spaghetti	134
Mashed Potatoes	135
Birista (Browned Onions)	135
Garam Masala	135

To Make A Good Jali (Lace)	135
Coconut Milk	136
To Prevent Curdling of Curds	137
To Boil Fish	137
To Tenderise Meat	137
Gelatine	138
How to Choose Vegetables	139
"Pretty" Cool	139
Deliciously Raw	140
Crisp and Tasty	140
The Secret of Puffy Egg Whites	141
Economy Drive	142
Souffle Hints	142
Glossary	144

In Loving Memory
of
Abdulla I. Rahimtoola
and
Amanullah M. Currim

JALEBI CARAMEL

¼ kg. jalebi	4 eggs
3 cups milk	1 tsp. rose essence
8 tbsp. sugar	¼ tsp. salt
4 tbsp. flour	A pat of butter

Take a flat bottomed baking dish and grease it well with butter. Heat the oven to 400°F.

Scald the milk. Beat the eggs lightly and add to the milk along with all the other ingredients except the jalebis. Beat thoroughly with a hand beater; or better still, in a blender for a minute. There should be no lumps.

Pour a thin layer of the mixture into the baking dish and let it set. Take out dish and arrange the jalebis in it. Pour the rest of the batter over the jalebis and bake at 400° for 35 to 40 minutes, till custard is set but moist. Reduce heat to 350° and bake for another 10 minutes so that custard is golden brown but not dry.

PINEAPPLE HALWA

One fully ripe pineapple, medium sized; when cleaned it should yield 1 kg. pineapple cubes	Good pinch saffron in 2 tbsp. hot water
400 gm. sugar	200 gm. plain mawa
½ cup water	200 gm. thick malai (or top of milk)
4 tbsp. ghee	A few blanched and chopped almonds

Make a thick syrup of the sugar and water (two strand) on a slow fire. Add the pineapple cubes to the syrup and simmer for about 20 minutes. The pineapple should be done and the syrup absorbed. Add saffron to this. Warm ghee and fry pineapple mixture in it, taking care not to burn pineapple pieces. Add mawa, roast, for three minutes, stirring continuously. Take off from fire, cool a little. Serve warm, garnished with malai and almond.

POTATO HALWA

1 kg. potatoes
½ kg. sugar
½ cup water
200 gm. plain mawa
200 gm. ghee
Good pinch saffron

2 tbsp. water
Powdered elaichi

Boil, peel and mash potatoes. Warm saffron and add it to 2 tbsp. water. Make a thick syrup (two strand) of the sugar and water on a slow fire.

Heat ghee and lightly fry the mashed potatoes. Mix saffron water into syrup, then add potatoes and cook, stirring continuously. Add mawa, mixing it in well. Cook for five minutes and take off from fire. Spread out on large plate, level, and sprinkle with elaichi.

Serve hot.

BREAD HALWA

½ kg. loaf of bread
4 large spoons of ghee
½ kg. sugar
3 cups milk
Some raisins

200 gm. mawa
Chopped nuts
200 gm malai or top
   of milk

Cut up loaf of bread into cubes. Fry cubes in the ghee. Heat the milk with the sugar and then add the bread cubes and raisins, and simmer till milk is absorbed. Lastly add the mawa, stirring it in well. Cook for five minutes. Take off from fire and pour into dish. Serve warm with a garnish of chopped nuts and malai.

STUFFED APPLES

6 to 8 large apples
¼ cup milk
1 cup sugar
¼ kg. plain mawa
50 gm. chopped kajus
Few raisins

A dash of cinnamon
   powder
200 gm. malai or thick top
   of milk

Cut off top of each apple and core it carefully, without piercing the other side.

Heat the milk and sugar, take off from fire and stir in mawa. Mix in the kajus, raisins and cinnamon and simmer to a thick pulp. Fill each apple with this mixture and cover top with malai. Bake in a moderate oven (350°) for half an hour, till the apples are tender.

If liked, colour the stuffing with a few drops of green colour.

PANEER DELIGHT

400 gm. paneer	½ tsp. baking soda
2 cups curds	4 eggs
200 gm. dairy cream	½ cup+2 tbsp. castor sugar
1 tsp. vanilla essence	
Juice and grated rind of 2 sour limes	One round, deep baking dish
2½ tbsp. cornflour	Fruit for garnish

Separate the egg yolks and whites. Beat yolks with ½ cup sugar till thick and lemon coloured.

Sieve paneer into mixing bowl. Add beaten yolks, curds, cream and all other ingredients except egg white and 2 tbsp. sugar. Whisk all the ingredients in a blender for a minute. Otherwise, beat thoroughly with wooden spoon. Beat egg whites until they hold soft peaks. Add the sugar and continue beating till they form stiff peaks but are moist. Stir in two tablespoons into above mixture and then fold in the rest of the whites. Pour into dish and bake for 1¾ hours in a slow oven at 250°. Switch off oven and do not remove the dish till cool.

Serve decorated with pineapple cubes and crushed peanuts, or slices of apple and orange.

LASAN KHEEMA

Bunch green garlic
1 kg. mince
2 tbsp. oil
1 chopped onion
2 cups hot water
Little ground ginger and chillies
1 tsp. dhania
1 tsp. jeera powder
½ tsp. red chilli powder
1 lemon
Few eggs (one per person)
½ cup ghee
Salt to taste

Fry onion, add ground masala and then kheema, fry. Add two cups hot water and cook the kheema. Remove from fire when water has dried out. Put the kheema in a big lagan or deep thali. Spread out evenly. Chop garlic very fine and sprinkle over kheema along with jeera and chilli powders. Squeeze lemon over it all. Then break eggs one by one and spread over kheema. Make the ghee piping hot and pour over the eggs. Do not stir but tilt the vessel so that eggs are covered with the ghee and cooked. Then strain off extra ghee and serve for an early morning breakfast in the cold season.

DRY GOSHT MASALA

½ kg. diced meat
Salt
4 tbsp. oil
1 tbsp. chopped coriander
1 tsp. garam masala powder
2 bay leaves
8 cloves ground garlic
¼" ground ginger
¼ tsp. turmeric
1 tsp. coriander|cummin seed powder
½ tsp. chilli powder

Boil the meat and dry water completely. Heat oil, fry bay leaves, then add all the spices (except garam masala and salt). Fry for a minute, then add meat, and fry well till the oil appears on top. Sprinkle chopped coriander and garam masala on top whilst serving.

BHUNA GOSHT

- 1 kg. beef undercut
- 4 tbsp. butter
- 2 tbsp. chilli powder
- Salt
- 1 tsp. ground garlic
- 1 tbsp. ground pomegranate seeds
- ½ tsp. ground ginger
- 2 tbsp. ground raw papaya (with skin)

Garnish: onion rings, lemon slices, mint leaves.

Cut meat in small cubes, marinate in all the ingredients for 2-3 hours. Put 8 pieces onto each greased skewer and grill on a slow charcoal fire till done. Put into serving dish, and arrange garnish on top.

RAILWAY MUTTON CURRY

½ kg. mutton (cut in small pieces and boiled)
1 grated onion
8 curry leaves
1 cup meat stock
Milk of ½ coconut
2 potatoes, peeled and cut in small pieces
3 tbsp. ghee
¼ cup amli water
Salt

Grind ½ coconut, 8 red chillies, 1 tsp. cummin seeds, 2 tbsp. coriander seeds, 7 cloves garlic, ½" ginger, salt, 1 tbsp. curry powder.

Fry onions and curry leaves in hot ghee till light brown, add ground spices and fry, then add stock. When it boils, add meat, potatoes and coconut milk. Cook gently till potatoes are done. Add amli water and salt last.

BENGALI FISH CURRY

1 kg. cleaned & cut fish (any kind)
4 med. size onions sliced
1 cup beaten curds
1 tsp. sugar
Salt
4 plums (alloo bhokharas)
¼ tsp. ground turmeric
6 tbsp. mustard oil

Grind 8 cloves garlic, 6 green chillies, ½" ginger, ½ tsp. salt, ¼ tsp. turmeric, ½ tsp. cummin seeds.

Heat oil, fry fish till brown and remove. In the

same oil, fry onions brown, put in the ground spices, and fry well. Add curds, turmeric, sugar and plums. Stir once, add salt and fish. Simmer uncovered for 5-7 minutes. Serve with boiled rice.

SHRIMP AND CORN BAKE

2 cups boiled shrimps	2 tbsp. flour
1 cup tinned corn	2 beaten eggs
½ ltr. milk	½ cup grated cheese
3 tbsp. butter	Salt

Cut finely: 4 green chillies, ¼ bunch mint, ¼ bunch coriander leaves.

Heat butter, fry flour till pink, add milk and stir till a thick smooth consistency is formed. Remove from fire, add salt, cheese, corn, shrimps, chillies, mint and coriander leaves. Lastly fold in beaten eggs. Pour into a greased dish, stand dish in a pan of hot water, and bake in a moderate oven (350°F) for half an hour. Serve with hot dinner rolls and a green salad.

MULLIGATAWNY MUTTON

½ kg. boiled mutton	Juice of 1 lemon
½ kg. boiled breast of mutton (seena ka gosht)	2 cups milk of 1 coconut
	2 tbsp. ghee
Salt	½ cup masoor dhal
6 curry leaves	

Grind 3 green chillies, 3 red chillies, ½ tbsp. turmeric, 1 tbsp. coriander, 1 tsp. cummin seeds, ½" ginger, 6 cloves garlic, 1 tsp. mustard seeds, 1 tsp. fenugreek seeds, 2 medium onions.

Boil dhal with 2 cups water and when soft, whisk till smooth. Heat ghee, fry curry leaves, then fry ground spices well. Add the meat, dhal and coconut milk and bring to the boil. Simmer for 15 mins. Remove from fire, and add lemon juice. Serve with boiled rice.

KHEEMA MASALA TUKRE

¼ kg. boiled mince
1 cup stock from boiled mince
4 eggs
Salt

Some chopped mint and coriander leaves
2 tbsp. any brown sauce
1 tsp. garam masala powder

Grind ¼ coconut, 4 green chillies, ½ tsp. cummin seeds, 6 cloves garlic, ¼" ginger, ¼ bunch coriander leaves.

In a greased dish put the mince mixed with stock, salt, brown sauce, ground spices, mint, coriander leaves and garam masala powder. Beat the eggs well, pour over the mince and bake in moderate oven (350°F) for 15-20 mins. or till set. Cut into squares or diamonds.

POTATO AND CORN ROLLS

1 cup mashed potatoes
1 large loaf of bread
1 cup boiled corn
Juice of 1 lemon
Salt

Oil to fry
Finely cut mint and coriander leaves
Finely chopped green chillies (to taste)

Mix potatoes, corn, salt, lemon juice, mint, coriander and chillies well together.

Dip bread slices in salted water, squeeze out water and form into rolls after filling potato mixture in the centre. Fry in hot oil till brown. Green peas may be used instead of corn.

WHITE MUTTON CURRY

$\frac{1}{2}$ kg. cut and boiled meat
1 cup stock
1 cup coconut milk (extracted from $\frac{1}{2}$ coconut)
Juice of 1 lemon
2 grated onions
10 curry leaves

1 tsp whole mixed spices (cloves, cinnamons, cardamoms, peppercorns)
2 peeled and quartered potatoes
3-4 tbsp. ghee
Salt

Grind $\frac{1}{2}$ coconut, 6 green chillies, 8 cloves garlic, $\frac{1}{2}''$ ginger, 1 tbsp. coriander seeds, 1 tbsp. poppy seeds, 1 tbsp. sesame seeds, 10 cashewnuts, 10 blanched almonds.

In hot ghee, put onions, curry leaves and whole spices. Fry for a few minutes, then add ground spices and fry well, adding stock gradually. Then add meat, potatoes and coconut milk. Simmer till potatoes are cooked. Add lemon juice and salt last (chopped mint and coriander leaves may be added if desired).

MUTTON MASALA SLICES

¼ kg. mutton
1 cup salad oil
Salt
1 tsp. each ground garlic and ginger
3 tbsp. Worcestershire sauce
1 tsp. chilli powder
3 tbsp. ghee
¼ kg. boiled peas
¼ kg. small tomatoes
½ kg. peeled, boiled potatoes

Cut the meat into slices and marinate it in salad oil, salt, garlic, ginger, Worcestershire sauce and chilli powder for at least four hours.

Heat ghee, put in meat, cover tightly (preferably with a weight on the lid) and cook on each side for 7 minutes. Remove meat and place in a serving dish. In the same gravy, fry peas, potatoes and tomatoes one by one, and spread over meat just before serving.

SPECIAL PUREES

1½ cups white flour (maida)
1 cup mashed potatoes
½ cup curds
Salt
Oil to fry

Sift flour into a bowl, add salt and potatoes and mix well. Then stir in curds and mix well, adding enough water to form a soft, non-sticky dough. Roll out in small rounds and fry in hot oil till lightly browned on both sides.

MINCE STEAKS

½ kg. mince
1 tsp. salt
½ tsp. pepper
1 cup fresh bread crumbs
1 egg yolk

1 onion
½ cup sifted flour
Ghee for frying
½ cup milk

Grate the onion, squeeze out the juice and strain it. Mix bread crumbs in milk, mix into mince with salt, pepper, onion juice and egg yolk. Keep for 2 hours. Form into 8 portions, shape into thick cutlets, dip into the plain flour and deep fry in ghee slowly until browned. Serve on a flat dish with a border of chips all round, dot each cutlet with chilli sauce and garnish with peas.

DUBALO CHAVAL

½ kg. minced meat
3 medium brinjals sliced
½ tsp. each ground ginger and garlic
Salt
2 med. onions cut
3 tbsp. oil

Chopped mint and coriander leaves
1½ cups water (strained from boiled rice)
1 piece cinnamon
4 cloves
6 peppercorns

Fry the cinnamon, cloves and peppercorns in hot oil, add onions and brown them. Add mince, ginger, garlic and salt and fry well. Add $\frac{3}{4}$ cup hot water (plain) and cook for 15 minutes. Add the brinjals and rice water and simmer till brinjals are done. Add mint and coriander. Serve with boiled rice.

KHURDI-KITCHRI

½ kg. meat, cut into pieces
Salt
2 tbsp. oil

4 cups water
2 tbsp. flour
Some cut mint leaves

Grind 6 cloves garlic, 3 green chillies, ¼" ginger, salt. Baghar: 1 tsp. cummin seed, 4 cloves chopped garlic, 2 sticks cinnamon, 4 cloves, 4 cardamons.

Rub the meat with ground spices and salt and keep for an hour. Mix the flour and water and cook the meat in it till done. Put in mint leaves. In a frying pan, heat oil and brown the baghar. Pour onto meat, and cover with lid. Serve with yellow kitchri.

KITCHRI

1 cup rice
1/3 cup masoor dhal
¼ tsp. turmeric
Salt
1 sliced onion (small)
1 bay leaf

2 cloves
2 peppercorns
2 cardamoms
1 stick cinnamon
2 tbsp. oil
2 whole red chillies

Heat oil, fry whole spices, chillies and the bay leaf: add onion and fry till brown. Add the washed rice and dhal, salt and turmeric. Fry for 2-3 minutes. Add 2½-3 cups hot water. Cook till the water almost dries, then cover with a lid and cook on a low fire till the rice is dry.

KUDAL PALIDU

1 cup cooked rice	1 minced onion
½ cup toover dhal	3 peeled and cut drum sticks or
Salt	
¼ tsp. turmeric	¼ kg. peeled and cut white pumkin
2-3 cups hot water	
2 tbsp. gram flour (besan)	3 kokums
3-4 tbsp. oil	
1 tsp. cummin seeds	
½ tsp. fenugreek seeds	

Grind 4 cloves garlic, ¼" ginger, 1 green chilli.

Boil the dhal in turmeric and water till soft. Strain and set aside dhal, and when the dhal-water is cool, mix in the gram flour and salt. Heat oil, fry cummin and fenugreek seeds. Add onion and fry till brown. Add ground spices and fry. Add vegetable and fry well; add the water with gram flour and bring to the boil. Simmer gently till the vegetable is cooked and liquid is thick; add kokums. Boil once. Spread dhal over the boiled rice and serve with above gravy.

SAFED PAYAS (TROTTERS)

9 trotters
4 onions
½ cup milk
Some mint leaves
3 tbsp. ghee

6 cloves garlic
1 tsp. cummin seeds
4 whole green chillies

Clean and cut the trotters and boil them with 6 cups of hot water and chopped onions. Sieve the liquid. Return the trotters to the liquid and boil again. Heat ghee, brown garlic, cummin seeds and green chillies and pour over the trotters. Cover and remove from heat. Cool for 5 minutes; add milk and mint leaves. Serve with tanduri roti.

To pressure cook use half the amount of water.

KHEEMA KAWABS

½ kg. mince
½ cup curds
Juice of 1 lemon
8 almonds or cashew nuts ground
¾ tsp. garam masala powder

Salt
1 med. onion ground
½" ginger ground
2-3 tbsp. ghee

Garnish: Mint leaves, onion rings and lemon slices.
Drain the curds in a cloth till dry. Mix all the ingredients with the curds except the ghee. Marinate for 2 hours. Make into long kababs (seekhs) onto skewers, tie up with thread and grill on a charcoal fire, basting with little ghee whilst grilling.

CHIKOLI CHAVAL

½ kg. cut meat or mince
¼ kg. mixed vegetables (small onions, small tomatoes, small potatoes, peas, chopped carrots and french beans)
Birista of 2 large onions
2 tbsp. oil
1 tbsp. ground ginger, garlic and green chilli

6 cloves chopped garlic
Salt
2 fairly large chapattis flavoured and rolled out, but not cooked, made from 150 gm. flour, 1 tbsp. ghee, ¼ tsp. haldi, ½ tsp. chilli powder, 1 tsp. salt

Put mince, salt, ground masala and all the vegetables (except tomatoes) in a pan with hot water (6 cups) and simmer till meat is done. Add the tomatoes and the chikoli dough cut into small diamond-shaped pieces. Add a little hot water if needed. Simmer till the chikoli is cooked. Heat oil, fry garlic till brown, and pour over contents of pan. Sprinkle birista on top and serve with boiled rice.

FISH SALAN (RED)

1 pomfret (cut into slices)
1 large onion finely minced
6 kokums
Salt
Thick milk of ¼ coconut

¼ bunch chopped coriander leaves
3 tbsp. oil
1½ tbsp. millet flour (mixed smooth in ¼ cup of water)

Grind 8 red chillies, 8 cloves garlic, 1 tbsp. dhania, 1 tbsp. cummin seeds, 6 curry leaves, ¼ tsp. turmeric, ¼ coconut, salt.

Heat oil, fry onions till pink in colour, add ground spices and fry well for 5 minutes. Add the coconut milk. When it boils, put in the millet paste, and stir well. Simmer for 5 minutes, add kokums and coriander leaves and simmer 10 minutes longer. Add salt and fish and cook 5 more minutes. Serve with kitchri or with millet rotis.

FISH CURRY (GREEN)

1 cleaned pomfret or 2 cups shelled prawns
1 large minced onion
8 curry leaves
Thick milk of 1 coconut
Salt
Juice of 1-2 lemons
1 tbsp. millet flour (mixed in ¼ cup water)
3 tbsp. oil
3-4 drumsticks (cut into quarters and boiled)

Grind 6 green chillies, ½ bunch coriander leaves, 1 tsp. aniseed, 8 cloves garlic, salt, 2 tbsp. curry powder.

Heat oil, fry onion and curry leaves till onion is pink in colour. Add ground spices and fry well. Put in coconut milk and when it boils, add millet flour. Stir well and simmer for 10 minutes. Put in the fish, drumsticks and salt and simmer 5 minutes longer. Add lemon juice to taste before serving.

Serve with kitchri or millet roti.

COCONUT MILK STEW

- ¼ kg. meat
- ¼ kg. chops
- 6 kidneys (halved)
- ½ tsp. ground garlic
- ½ tsp. ground ginger
- 2 med. onions minced
- 4 stalks celery cut into 1" pieces
- ½ cup shelled peas
- 6 slit green chillies
- 3 tbsp. oil
- Thick milk of 1 coconut (mixed smooth with 2 tbsp. white flour)
- 8 tiny tomatoes
- 8 tiny potatoes (peeled)
- 8 tiny onions (peeled)
- 2 small sticks cinnamon
- 6 cloves
- 10 peppercorns
- 4 cardamoms

Boil the meat and kidneys with the garlic, ginger and some salt. Heat oil, fry whole spices, then fry minced onions and green chillies. When onion is transparent, add celery, meat stock, salt, peas, small whole onions and potatoes. Boil once, add coconut milk, and simmer uncovered till potatoes are done. Add in meat and tomatoes. Simmer 5 minutes longer and serve with boiled rice or bread.

MOONG CURRY

- 1 cup moong dhal or whole (boiled and 1 cup water kept)
- Salt
- 4 kokums
- ¼ tsp. turmeric
- ½ tsp chilli powder
- 2 tbsp. chopped coriander leaves
- 1 cup thick coconut milk (mixed with 1 tbsp. channa flour)
- 2 tbsp. oil
- 6 cloves crushed garlic
- ½ tsp. cummin seeds
- 8 curry leaves
- 3 cut green chillies

Heat oil, fry the garlic, cummin seeds, curry leaves and chillies till brown. Add in moong and water. When it boils, put in salt, turmeric, chilli powder and kokums. Simmer for 5 minutes, add coconut milk and coriander. Stir continuously till it starts boiling Remove from fire, serve with rice.

WHITE PUMPKIN DHAL

1 cup toover dhal	½ kg. white pumpkin
1 cup masoor dhal	(peeled and cut)
2 onions	½ cup imli water
Salt	1 tbsp. each chopped mint
2 tbsp. oil	and coriander leaves
¼ tsp. turmeric	8 curry leaves
4 tbsp. ghee	6 cloves crushed garlic

Grind 6 red chillies, 8 cloves garlic, ¼ tsp. turmeric, 1 tsp. cummin seeds, 1 tbsp. dhania, salt, 1 tbsp. dessicated coconut, ½ tsp. garam masala powder.

Boil both dhals with one minced onion, salt, oil and turmeric, then sieve them. Heat half the ghee and fry one sliced onion till well browned. Add ground spices and when well fried, add white pumpkin. Fry for 3-5 minutes, add 2-3 cups hot water, cover and simmer till pumpkin is soft. Add dhal to this, and the amli water, salt, mint and coriander. Simmer for 10 minutes. In a small pan heat remaining ghee, fry curry leaves and crushed garlic till brown, add to dhal and quickly cover pan. Leave covered on slow fire for 10 minutes. Serve with fried rice or tandur roti.

PALAK GOSHT (MEAT WITH SPINACH)

½ kg. cut mutton
4 bunches chopped spinach
3 tbsp. ghee
1 large minced tomato
1 med. minced onion
Salt

½ tsp. garam masala powder
2 tbsp. white butter

Grind 6 cloves garlic, ½" ginger, 2 green chillies, 1 tsp. chilli powder, ¼ tsp. turmeric, 1 tsp. coriander/cummin seed powder.

Heat ghee, add in onion and fry till lightly browned, then add ground spices and fry for 2 minutes. Add meat and salt and brown meat well. Add 2 cups hot water. Cover and simmer till meat is done. Put in spinach and tomato, and simmer till water dries. Uncover pan and fry contents well till thick. Serve with butter on top, and sprinkle with garam masala powder. Serve with parathas or tandur roti.

GREEN SHURWA

¼ kg. mutton
¼ kg. breast of mutton (seene ka gosht)
1 tsp. ground garlic
1 tsp. ground ginger
1 large minced onion
2 tbsp. ghee
Salt
1 large ground onion

2 med. unpeeled, cut potatoes
Juice of 1 lemon
1 stick cinnamon
3 cloves
3 cardamoms

Grind ½ med. bunch of coriander, ¼ tsp. turmeric, 6 green chillies.

Boil meat with garlic, ginger, minced onion and salt till 2 cups stock remain. In ghee, fry spices brown, then add ground onion, fry till pink. Fry the ground spices for 2-3 minutes, add the meat with its stock. Add the potatoes and simmer till done. Add lemon juice.

Serve with boiled rice or kitchri.

RED SHURWA

½ kg. cut mutton	2 tbsp. ghee
¼ kg. peeled and quartered potatoes	2 tbsp. chopped mint
2 large sliced onions	2 tbsp. chopped coriander
Salt	
¼ kg. peeled and ground tomatoes	

Grind 6 red chillies, 8 cloves garlic, ½" ginger.

Powder 1 stick cinnamon, 4 cloves, 4 cardamoms, 6 peppercorns.

Heat ghee, fry onions golden brown, add meat and fry well till brown. Then add ground spices and fry well. Add 4 cups water and cook till meat is tender. Add the remaining ingredients and more hot water if needed, and cook till potatoes are done and gravy slightly thickish.

Serve with boiled rice or kitchri.

MUTTON AND VEGETABLE SHURWA

- 1 kg. cleaned and cut mutton
- 1 cup shelled peas
- ¼ kg. peeled and cut potatoes
- Salt
- Milk of 1 coconut
- ¼ kg. cut tomatoes
- 1 small cauliflower (cut into sprigs)
- 3 tbsp. ghee
- 2 med. onions sliced
- 1 stick cinnamon
- 6 cloves
- 6 cardamoms
- 8 peppercorns

Grind 6 green chillies, 8 cloves garlic, ½" ginger, ½ bunch coriander.

Apply ground spices to meat, and keep aside for an hour. Heat ghee, fry the whole spices, add onions and meat, and fry well together till onion is soft. Add 3-4 cups hot water, and simmer till meat is tender. Add the tomatoes and when soft, put in the remaining vegetables (except potatoes), salt and coconut milk. Bring to boiling point; then simmer till the peas are half cooked. Add potatoes. Remove from heat when potatoes and peas are cooked. Serve with bread or boiled rice.

MUTTON DO PIAZA

- 1 kg. cleaned and cut mutton
- ¼ kg. sliced onions
- 4 tbsp. ghee
- Salt
- ½ cup beaten curds
- 8 red chillies, broken into small pieces
- 3 black cardamoms
- 8 peppercorns
- 6 cloves
- 2 sticks cinnamon
- 8 cloves finely cut garlic
- ½" finely cut ginger
- 4 cups hot water

Mix all ingredients except curds in a pan, cover with lid, and cook over medium heat till meat is done. Remove lid, add in the curds and fry well till brown. Serve with phulkas.

AB GOSHT (GREEN)

½ kg. cleaned and cut mutton
1 cup gram dhal
1 tsp. ground ginger
½ tsp. ground garlic
Salt
2 large minced onions
Juice of 2 lemons
½ tsp. turmeric

6 whole green chillies
2 tbsp. ghee
2 tbsp. oil
3 tbsp. chopped mint
2 cups coconut milk

Grind ½ bunch coriander, 4 green chillies, salt.
Powder 1 stick cinnamon, 6 cloves, 6 cardamoms, 8 peppercorns.
In a pan put meat, dhal, ground ingredients, turmeric, salt, onions, whole chillies, ginger, garlic and oil. Add 4 cups hot water, and cook gently till meat is done. Add coconut milk and mint, and cook uncovered for 10 minutes more. Heat ghee in a frying pan till very hot. Sprinkle spice powder on the meat, and pour hot ghee over it quickly, and cover for 2-3 minutes. Remove from heat and add lemon juice. Serve with tandur roti or boiled rice.

AB GOSHT (RED)

- ½ kg. cut mutton
- Milk of 1 coconut
- 3 tbsp. ghee
- Salt
- 1 large minced onion
- ¼ kg. minced tomatoes
- ½ cup gram dhal
- 4 whole green chillies
- 1 stick cinnamon
- 6 cloves
- 6 cardamoms
- 8 peppercorns
- 2 tbsp. cut mint
- 2 tbsp. cut coriander
- 6 curry leaves
- ½ tsp cummin seeds
- 4 cloves of garlic minced

Grind 8 red chillies, ½" ginger, 8 cloves garlic, salt, ¼ tsp. turmeric.

Boil the dhal and grind half of it. Heat ghee, fry the curry leaves, cummin seeds, garlic, whole spices and green chillies till brown. Add onion and fry till pinkish. Put in ground spices and meat and fry both together for 5 minutes. Add tomatoes and fry again till they are well mixed with the spices. Add 3 cups hot water, and cook covered till meat is done. Add the coconut milk, salt, whole and ground dhal, coriander and mint. Simmer for 15 minutes.

Serve with tandur roti or boiled rice.

SWEET 'N' SOUR MUTTON

- ½ kg. cleaned and cut mutton
- 10 cloves ground garlic
- 1" ground ginger
- Salt
- 4 tbsp. ghee
- 4 medium onions sliced
- 15 dried apricots (seeds removed and soaked in ¼ cup water)
- ½ cup vinegar mixed with 3 tbsp. sugar
- 2 large potatoes cut and fried
- 1 stick cinnamon
- 6 cloves
- 4 cardamoms
- 8 peppercorns
- 6 red chillies broken into halves

Heat ghee, fry the chillies and whole spices. Add onions, and when golden brown, add meat with ground garlic and ginger and brown well. Add 3 cups hot water, cover and cook over medium heat till meat is done. Add dried apricots, vinegar and salt and simmer for 5 minutes. Put in potatoes.

Serve with bread or chapattis.

CURRIED CORN

3 roasted cobs of corn	Salt
2 tbsp. ghee	Juice of 1-2 lemons
Milk of ½ coconut	

Grind ½ coconut, 6 green chillies, 1 tsp. cummin seeds, ¼ tsp. turmeric, 6 cloves garlic, salt, ½ bunch coriander.

Remove the corn from the cobs. Heat ghee, fry well and add coconut milk. As soon as it boils, add corn and cook till gravy is thick. Add salt to taste. Add lemon juice just before serving. (Instead of fresh roasted corn, tinned corn and its stock can be used).

BOTEE GOSHT SALAN

1 kg. mutton cut into small pieces	Salt
2 medium onions minced	2 large potatoes
2 large tomatoes	2 tbsp. cut coriander leaves
	3 tbsp. ghee

Grind 6 red chillies, 2 green chillies, ½ tsp. turmeric, 2 tbsp. coriander, 1 tsp. cummin seeds, 10 cloves garlic, ½" ginger.

Peel the potatoes, cut into cubes and fry them till light brown. Blanch the tomatoes and grind them. In ghee, fry onions till brown. Add the meat, fry well and then fry the ground spices. Add salt and 3 cups water. Cover and cook till meat is soft; add tomato pulp and cook uncovered till a thick gravy forms. Add potatoes. Sprinkle coriander on top before serving.

Serve with phulkas.

PEA POTATO MASALA

½ kg. peeled potatoes, cut into fingers
1 cup shelled peas
2 medium onions minced
4 tbsp. oil
Salt
½ tsp. mustard seeds
8 curry leaves
1 large minced tomato

Grind 6 cloves garlic, ¼ tsp. peppercorns, ¼" ginger, 2 tsp. coriander seeds, ¼ tsp. turmeric, 1 tsp. chilli powder.

Heat oil, fry curry leaves and mustard seeds; add onions and brown well. Fry the ground spices. Add tomatoes and fry till soft. Put in the peas and 1½ cups of hot water. When peas are half cooked, put in potatoes and salt and simmer covered till done.

Serve with phulkas.

HYDERABADI MASALA GOSHT

- ½ kg. diced mutton
- 1 sliced onion
- 8 cloves sliced garlic
- ½" sliced ginger
- 4 green chillies sliced
- ¼ kg. beaten curds
- 6 tbsp. ghee
- Salt
- ½ tsp. turmeric
- 6 peppercorns
- 2 sticks cinnamon
- 4 cloves
- 4 cardamoms

In a pan, melt 4 tablespoons of ghee. Remove from heat, mix in meat, curds, turmeric, salt, sliced ingredients and spices. Seal pan with flour paste and cook on medium heat for ½ hour. Open pan, add the remaining ghee and cook till the meat and spices turn a reddish brown. Serve with purees or parathas.

ALOO GOSHT

- ½ kg. diced mutton
- ¼ kg. peeled and cut potatoes
- 1 large sliced onion
- Salt
- 3 tbsp. ghee
- 2 tbsp. cut coriander
- ½ tsp. pepper powder

Grind ½ tsp. turmeric, 6 red chillies, 8 cloves garlic, 1 tsp. dhania, ½" ginger.

Brown onions in heated ghee; remove and grind to a paste with pepper. In same ghee, add ground spices and fry well. Put in meat and salt and fry for 3 minutes, then add 3 cups hot water and simmer till meat is cooked. Dry the stock by cooking on a fast fire. Add onion and potatoes, fry again for 2-3 minutes, add 2 cups hot water, and simmer till the potatoes are cooked. Sprinkle coriander on top.

Serve with naan or boiled rice.

CAULIFLOWER GOSHT

½ kg. cut meat
½ kg. cauliflower cut into medium-sized sprigs
1 large sliced onion
Salt

3 cut green chillies
2 tbsp. chopped dil leaves (soova bhaji)
3 tbsp. ghee

Grind ½ tsp. turmeric, 1½ tsp. coriander, 4 red chillies, ½" ginger, 8 cloves garlic.

Marinate the meat with the ground spices and keep for 2 hours. Heat ghee, fry onion till brown; add meat and salt, and fry well. Add 3 cups hot water, and cook covered till meat is tender. Add cauliflower and 1 cup hot water, and cook gently. Lastly add the green chillies and dil leaves and simmer for 5 minutes longer.

Serve with phulkas.

SHABH DEGH

½ kg. cut mutton
5 tbsp. ghee
Salt
½ kg. turnips, peeled and quartered
1 large sliced onion
1 cup beaten curds

4 cloves
4 cardamoms
1 stick cinnamon
2 tsp. kewra water
1½ tsp. sugar
1 tsp. lemon juice

Grind 1 large onion, ½" ginger, 2 tsp. chilli powder, 1 pod garlic, 3 tsp. coriander seeds.

Heat ghee, fry sliced onion till brown; remove and crush them. In the same ghee fry turnips till brown and remove them. Fry the meat till brown and remove this also. In the same pan add 1 more tablespoon ghee, if needed, and fry the cloves, cardamoms and cinnamon till brown. Add ground spices and brown. Add the meat, turnips, crushed onions and salt and fry till mixed well with spices Add the curds and 4 cups hot water. Simmer till meat is tender and 2 cups gravy left. Remove from fire and stir in kewra mixed with sugar and lemon juice. Serve with naan.

KABABI GOSHT

¾ kg. cut mutton	2 med. onions ground
4 tbsp. ghee	4 cloves
1 cup beaten curds	4 cardamoms
Salt	1 stick cinnamon
2 tsp. ground pepper	
1 tbsp. ground ginger	
1 tbsp. ground red chillies	

Heat ghee, brown whole spices; add chillies, onions, ginger and pepper and brown well. Add meat, curds, 2 cups hot water and salt. Simmer till meat is tender, then fry well till gravy is thick and dark brown. Serve with purees or parathas.

KATAY MASSALAY KA GOSHT

- ¼ kg. cut mutton
- 3 tbsp. ghee
- ¼ tsp. cummin seeds
- 1 stick cinnamon
- 4 big black cardamoms
- Salt
- 4 cloves
- 4 peppercorns
- ½ cup beaten curds

Slice finely ¼ kg. onion, 6 green chillies, 8 cloves garlic ½" ginger.

Mix all the spices, meat, salt, sliced ingredients and ghee well. Add 3 cups water, cover, and keep on a fast fire till it boils. Reduce heat and cook till meat is tender and water dry. Add curds and fry well till ghee appears on top. Serve with phulkas or purees.

KHEEMA KARELA

- ¼ kg. mince
- 4 tbsp. ghee
- ¼ kg. sliced onions
- ¼ kg. peeled and cut bitter gourd
- Salt
- 6 cloves ground garlic
- 2 tsp. chilli powder
- ¼ tsp. salt
- 1 tsp. coriander powder
- ½ tsp. turmeric

Mix garlic, chilli powder, salt, coriander powder and turmeric with ¼ cup water.

Apply salt to the bitter gourd and keep for 2 hours, then wash well. Heat ghee, fry the gourd till golden brown and remove. In the same ghee, fry onions till brown. Add mince and fry again for 5 minutes;

add the browned gourd and 2 cups hot water. Cook on medium heat till the mince is tender and water dries. Fry well till brown.

Serve with phulkas.

MURG TAMATAR

1 cleaned and cut chicken	2 tbsp. poppy seeds (ground in ¼ cup milk)
4 tbsp. ghee	
2 bay leaves	½ kg. blanched mashed tomatoes
Salt	
1 tsp. sugar	2 large grated onions

Grind 8 dry red chillies, 10 cloves garlic, ½" ginger, ¼ tsp. turmeric, salt.

Heat ghee, fry bay leaves and onions till pink. Add ground spices and fry for 2 minutes, then add chicken and fry well for 5 minutes. Put in tomato pulp, salt and sugar and cook on a slow fire (with lid on) till chicken is tender. Add poppy seeds, milk mixture and fry well for another 5 minutes. Serve with phulkas.

BIHARI GRILLED MEAT

½ kg. breast of mutton (seene ka gosht)	2 tbsp. ghee
¼ cup beaten curds	½ tsp. freshly ground pepper
Salt	

Cook mutton with curds, salt and 3 cups water, till tender and the water dries. Heat ghee in a frying pan, fry the meat with pepper sprinkled on top, till well browned.

Serve with a border of onion salad around meat, to be eaten with phulkas.

ONION SALAD

2 large minced onions
2 minced green chillies
Salt

Juice of 1 lemon
2 tbsp. chopped mint

Mix all ingredients well.

SHALGUM MUTTER VEGETABLE

½ kg. peas (shelled)
½ kg. grated turnips
1 grated onion
½ tsp. ground garlic
½ tsp. ground ginger
2 tbsp. oil or ghee
3 finely cut green chillies
Salt

Some chopped mint and coriander leaves
Juice of 1 lemon mixed with 1 tsp. sugar
¼ tsp. turmeric
½ tsp. chilli powder
1 tsp. coriander|cummin seed powder

Heat oil and fry the onion, garlic and ginger till pink. Add the peas and fry till light red in colour. Add green chillies, salt, turmeric, chilli powder and coriander/cummin seed powder and fry well. Add the turnips. Cover and cook on a slow fire till peas are done. Add lemon juice, mint and coriander leaves. Serve with hot phulkas.

YAKHNI PULAO

- 1 kg. mutton cut into big pieces
- ½ kg. breast of mutton (seene ka gosht)
- 1 tsp. ground ginger
- 1 tsp. ground garlic
- Salt
- 2 sticks cinnamon
- 8 cloves
- 10 peppercorns
- ½ tsp. caraway seeds
- 6 cardamoms
- 6 tbsp. ghee
- 2 tbsp. kewra water
- 3 bay leaves
- 3 medium sliced onions
- 1 kg. washed rice
- ½ kg. peeled and halved potatoes

Tie the whole spices in a cloth. Put the meat in a pan with 8 cups of water; add the spice bag. Simmer covered till the meat is tender. Remove meat from stock; also remove spice bag, squeeze out well and throw away. Heat ghee, fry bay leaves well, add onions and brown. Add the rice and fry well, add meat and potatoes and fry 5 more minutes. Add the stock and salt and boil till water is dry. Add more water and cook till rice is done; sprinkle kewra over rice.

Cover the pan with a wet cloth, and then cover with the lid. Keep on a slow fire for 15 minutes. Serve with raita (curd salad).

DHAL GOSHT

- ¼ cup channa dhal
- ¼ cup masoor dhal
- ¼ cup toovar dhal
- Salt
- 3 tbsp. ghee
- 2 tbsp. oil
- ¼ kg. boiled meat (keep 1-2 cups stock)
- ¼ tsp. garam masala powder
- 2 large finely chopped tomatoes
- 1 large sliced onion
- 2 bay leaves

Grind 4 red chillies, 4 green chillies, handful coriander leaves, 2 tbsp. curry powder, 2 tbsp. dessicated coconut, 8 curry leaves, 2 tsp. aniseed, 10-12 mint leaves, ¼ tsp. turmeric.

Boil the three types of dhal together and sieve them. Heat 2 tablespoon of oil and 1 tablespoon ghee, and fry onion till brown. Add ground spices and bay leaves and fry well. Add the salt and tomatoes, and fry till the tomatoes are soft (whilst frying add meat stock, a little at a time). Then add meat; fry this for 2 minutes, then put in dhal. Add 1 cup hot water if the consistency is too thick. Stir well and keep on low fire to simmer.

In a small pan heat 2 tablespoons of ghee till very hot. Remove from fire. Sprinkle garam masala on dhal, pour hot ghee over it and cover with lid for 3-5 minutes.

Serve with fried rice, onion salad and fried papads.

KONKANI SALAN

- ¼ kg. boiled meat
- 2 cups stock
- Salt
- 3 grated onions
- 4 unpeeled, quartered potatoes
- 3 tbsp. ghee
- ¼ tsp. saffron, heated and powdered
- ¾ tsps. powdered garam masala
- 1 tbsp. chopped coriander leaves

Grind 10 dry red chillies, 7 cloves garlic, 1 inch ginger, 2 tbsp. coriander, 1 tsp. cummin seed, ¼ dry coconut.

Fry onions in ghee till light brown, add ground spices and fry well. Add meat and stock; when it boils, add salt and unpeeled potatoes. Simmer till potatoes are done. Then add saffron and garam masala and remove from fire.

Serve with coriander leaves sprinkled on top.

PINEAPPLE CURRY

- 2 cups fresh pineapple cubes
- 2 tsp. sugar
- 2 medium minced onions
- 2 tbsp. oil
- Milk of 1 coconut
- 2 tbsp. channa flour (mixed in ¼ cup water)
- Salt
- ¼ tsp. turmeric
- 6 curry leaves
- 6 whole red chillies

Put pineapple in pan with sugar and 3 cups water. Simmer till soft. Mix in turmeric, salt, coconut milk and channa flour and stir well. In another pan, heat oil and fry curry leaves, red chillies and onions. When light brown add to curry.

Simmer for 5 minutes longer.

PHALLI BESAN

6 drumsticks (cut into 3-inch pieces and boiled)
2 medium chopped tomatoes
3 tbsp. oil
2 tbsp. channa flour (mixed in ¼ cup water)
Salt
¼ tsp. turmeric
1 tsp. chilli powder
Walnut-size lump of jaggery
½ tsp. mustard seeds
8 curry leaves

Heat oil, add mustard seeds and curry leaves and fry till brown. Put in tomatoes and salt and fry till tomatoes are soft. Add turmeric, chilli powder and jaggery. When the jaggery dissolves, put in the boiled drumsticks and the stock (if any). When boiling add channa flour and stir continuously till thick.

ROTI SALAN

1 kg. mutton
½ tsp. ginger
½ tsp. garlic
6 cups meat stock
Salt
2 cups finely cut left-over chapattis
2 chicken or meat soup cubes
½ tsp. pepper
Birista of 2 large onions
2 tbsp. oil
6 cloves crushed garlic
1 large bay leaf (quartered)
4 red chillies (broken into quarters)
1 tsp. cummin seeds

Garnish: chopped mint, lemon juice, browned onion slices.

Boil the meat with the ginger and garlic. Fry the garlic, bay leaf, chillies and cummin seeds in hot oil till brown. Add meat stock and bring to the boil. Put in soup cubes, salt, pepper and birista. Simmer for 5 minutes, then add meat and chappatties. Cook till the chappaties absorb the liquid, but do not allow it to get too dry.

Serve in soup bowls with some mint, and browned onions sprinkled on top; add a few drops of lemon juice to taste.

LUCKNOWI TAMATAR GOSHT

1 kg. cut mutton	3-4 cups hot water
100 gm. ground tomatoes	1 tsp. ground garlic
3 tbsp. oil	1 tsp. ground ginger
Salt	

Grind (after roasting) 2 large onions, 1 tsp. gingelly seeds, 1 tsp. poppy seeds, 6 red chillies, 1 stick cinnamon, 6 cloves, 8 peppercorns.

Heat oil and fry meat with ginger, garlic and salt. When well browned add hot water and simmer with lid on, till meat is tender. Dry the water by cooking on a fast fire without lid. Put in ground spices and continue to fry well, after spices become reddish brown. Add tomatoes, and fry again for 5 minutes.

MEAT IN TANDUR ROTI

½ kg. boiled mutton
2 cups soup
Salt
2 minced onions
1 tbsp. vinegar
1 tbsp. Worcestershire sauce
2 tbsp. ghee

¼ kg. curds
1 cut-up tandur roti
½ tsp. mixed spices (cloves, cinnamon, cardamoms, peppercorns)
Few mint leaves
½ tsp. chilli powder

Grind 6 green chilies, 8 cloves garlic, 1" ginger, ½ bunch coriander leaves.

Heat ghee, fry onions and whole spices light brown; add ground spices and fry well. Put in meat and soup. When it boils, add salt, vinegar and sauce. Boil once. Put in roti and remove from heat when it has absorbed all the gravy. Put in a serving dish and spread beaten curds over the top. Garnish with mint leaves and chilli powder.

LUCKNOWI BHUNA GOSHT

- 1 kg. cut mutton
- 2 large sliced onions
- Salt
- 1 tsp. ground ginger
- 1 tsp. ground garlic
- ½ kg. peeled, ground tomatoes
- 3 tbsp. chopped coriander
- 1 tsp. garam masala powder
- 4 tbsp. ghee
- ½ tsp. turmeric
- 1 tsp. chilli powder
- 1 tsp. coriander powder
- ½ tsp. cummin powder

Heat ghee, and fry onions till light brown. Add meat, ginger, garlic and salt and fry well for 5 minutes. Add turmeric, chilli, coriander and cummin powders and brown 3 more minutes. Add 3 cups hot water, and cook till meat is tender. Now add tomato, chopped coriander and garam masala powder, and fry well till it turns a rich reddish brown colour or till the ghee appears on top.

Serve with purees or parathas.

ZANZIBAR FISH CURRY

- 1 large cleaned and cut pomfret
- 3 green chillies
- Salt
- 4 cloves garlic
- 1 sprig of mint
- 4 cloves
- 6 peppercorns
- Milk of 1 coconut
- 1 tbsp. flour
- 2 tbsp. ghee or oil
- 2 lemons

Boil the fish with salt, chillies, garlic, mint, cloves, peppercorns and the juice of one lemon. Keep 1 cup strained stock in which fish has been boiled. Heat ghee or oil, fry flour for 1 minute, add stock and stir till it boils. Add coconut milk and boil again till thickish gravy is formed. Carefully put in fish and lemon juice. Remove from the fire.

Serve with boiled rice or bread.

TOMATO EGG CURRY

2 minced onions
1 kg. tomatoes
3 tbsp. ghee
Salt
Juice of 1 lemon
Milk of 1 coconut
1 tsp. flour
6 hard-boiled eggs

¼ tsp. heated and powdered saffron
1 tbsp. sugar

Grind 10 red chillies, 7 cloves garlic, 1 tsp. cummin seeds, 10 peppercorns, ¼ dry coconut, 3 tbsp. coriander.

Blanch the tomatoes and mash them. Heat ghee, fry onions light brown; add ground spices and fry well. Then add the tomato pulp. Mix the flour into the coconut milk and pour over the pulp. Add saffron and simmer for 10 minutes. Add salt, lemon juice, sugar and eggs just before removing from fire.

PASANDE KABABS

- 1 kg. mutton (sliced lengthwise)
- 3 large sliced onions
- 2 tbsp. poppy seeds
- 1 tsp. peppercorns
- 1 tsp. garam masala (whole)
- 10 cloves garlic
- ¼" ginger
- 8 red chillies
- ¼ dry coconut chopped
- 3 tbsp. ghee
- Salt
- 2 tbsp. ground raw papaya (with skin)
- 4 tbsp. ghee

Heat 2 tbsp. ghee, fry onions, poppy seeds, peppercorns, chillies, coconut, ginger, garlic and whole garam masala till well browned. Remove from heat, drain off ghee and grind to a paste. Apply to meat slices with salt and papaya and keep for 3 to 4 hours. Roll up each slice tightly and tie up with thread. Heat the remaining ghee in a frying pan, put in all the kababs, and cook on a medium fire, shaking pan gently from side to side till kababs are done. Serve with onion and lemon rings.

KAKOWRI-KE-KABABS

- ½ kg. mince
- 1 tsp raw, unpeeled, ground papaya
- Salt
- 1 tsp. garam masala powder
- 2 tbsp. ghee
- 3 tbsp. roasted, peeled gram
- Birista of 2 large onions

Mix the papaya with mince and keep for 1 hour. Pound the gram, and mix into the mince with garam masala. Keep for 1 hour more. Apply water to hand and shape the mince onto skewers. Roast over a charcoal fire for 5 minutes, turning slowly around. On another fire, keep a frying pan with warm (not hot) ghee: put in the kababs, shake pan gently from side to side, so as not to break the kababs. Serve at once, with birista and lemon rings and a hot chutney.

HOT CHUTNEY

Grind together 4 red chillies, 4 green chillies, ½ tsp salt, 1 medium onion, 1 tsp. dry pomegranate seeds 1 tsp. cummin seeds, ¼ bunch coriander leaves.*

DAHI MEAT

½ kg. mutton	1" finely sliced ginger
½ kg. curds (beaten)	6 finely sliced green chillies
Salt	6 cloves garlic sliced
2 minced onions	2 tbsp. ghee
½ bunch coriander leaves	1 tsp. garam masala powder

Marinate meat in beaten curds for 4-5 hours. Heat ghee. Fry onions till brown. Then add meat and fry well till half done. Then add the ginger, garlic, salt, chillies and coriander leaves. Cook till meat is soft and water dries. Sprinkle garam masala whilst serving.

* See p. 133 "Helpfully Yours"

PUNJABI CHOLE

1 cup kabuli channa
¼ kg. boiled, peeled and cut potatoes
1 tsp. cardamom powder
Salt

3 tbsp. oil
1 tbsp. dry mango powder
1 tbsp. each of cut mint and coriander leaves

Cut finely ½" ginger, 1 medium onion, 8 green chillies, 8 cloves garlic.

Soak the kabuli channa overnight in 3 cups water, with ¼ tsp. soda in it. Boil or pressure cook in the same water till very soft. Heat oil, fry the cut ingredients till light brown. Add salt, mango powder, and cardamom powder. Fry for a minute and add kabuli channa with the water, potatoes, mint and coriander. Simmer covered for 15 minutes. Serve with special maida purees.

DAHI CHOPS

1 kg. mutton chops
2 cups beaten curds
Salt
1 tbsp. poppy seeds
10 cashewnuts
¼ cup milk
3 tbsp. ghee
Handful cut coriander leaves

½ tsp. shahzeera (caraway seeds)
½ tsp. peppercorns
2 sticks cinnamon
6 cloves
6 cardamoms

Grind 3 medium-sized onions, 6 red chillies, ¼ tsp. turmeric, ½ tsp. salt, 8 cloves garlic, ½" ginger.

Grind the poppy seeds and cashewnuts with the milk. In ghee, put whole spices, then add chops and ground spices together and fry well for 5 minutes. Add the curds and salt and cook uncovered till chops are tender. Then add the poppyseed, cashewnut paste, and cook till ghee appears on top. Garnish with coriander leaves whilst serving.

Serve with phulkas or purees.

PASANDE

½ kg. mutton
3 minced onions
Salt
¼ kg. beaten curds
2 tbsp. ghee
1 tsp. garam masala powder

3 unpeeled, sliced potatoes
10 ground almonds
1 cup meat stock or water

Grind (after roasting on a griddle) 8 cloves garlic, ½" ginger, 8 red chillies, 1 tbsp. coriander seeds, 1 tbsp. poppy seeds, ¼ tsp. peppercorns.

Cut the meat into lengthwise slices; then boil it, adding only salt. Heat ghee, fry onions light brown, add potatoes and ground spices and fry well. Add stock or water and cook till potatoes are done. Add meat, curds and garam masala. When it starts boiling, put in almonds. Cook till gravy is thick.

SEEKH CURRY

- ½ kg. mutton (cubed and boiled)
- 2 peeled, boiled and cubed potatoes
- 2 cubed onions
- 2 tbsp. ghee
- Salt
- ¼ cup beaten curds
- 1 large ground tomato
- 1 minced onion
- ½ tsp. garam masala powder

Grind 2 red chillies, 1 green chilli, 3 cloves garlic, ¼" ginger, ¼ tsp. salt, ¼ bunch of coriander leaves.

Skewer pieces of meat, onion and potatoes on cleaned sticks. In ghee fry minced onions light brown, add ground spices and fry. Then put in tomato and stir well; add curds and salt (if needed) and gently put in skewered meat. Boil once, add garam masala powder, then remove from fire. Serve with mashed potatoes, bread or chapattis.

SHAMI KABABS

- ½ kg. meat (minced)
- 3 tbsp. channa dhal
- 1 cut onion
- 3 red chillies
- 4 cloves garlic
- 1" ginger
- 1 tsp. aniseed
- 2 tsp. dhania
- 1 tsp. whole garam masala
- 1½ cups water
- 1 tbsp. poppy seeds
- ½ tsp. salt

All the above ingredients to be boiled together till water dries.

- 1 egg
- Ghee or oil to fry

Filling: 3 green chillies, 1 onion, mint, coriander leaves; all to be cut finely.

Grind the mince and other boiled ingredients very finely. Mix in the egg, make into small cutlets, and fill with the finely chopped ingredients. Fry in very little ghee or oil till well browned. Drain on paper before serving.

KADDU CHANNA

2 cups channa dhal
2 large sliced onions
1 kg. peeled and chopped pumpkin
3 tbsp. ghee
1 tbsp. roasted and powdered cummin seeds
½ tsp. pepper, freshly powdered
Salt

Grind 8 red chillies, ½ tsp. turmeric, salt, 8 cloves garlic, 1 tbsp. coriander, ½" ginger.

Soak dhal for 3 hours, boil with pumpkin till dhal is soft, and keep aside. In ghee, brown onions, add the ground spices, cummin seed powder and pepper, and fry well. Put in some water if needed, and taste for salt. Simmer for 10-15 minutes. Serve with phulkas

BAIDE KI-ROTI

2 cups plain flour
¼ kg. ghee
4-5 eggs
1 minced onion
Salt
3 minced green chillies
½ kg. mince boiled dry
1 tbsp. flour
Some chopped coriander leaves

Bind the flour to a smooth dough with ¼ tsp. salt and warm water and keep for 1 hour. Mix the mince, onions, chillies, salt and coriander leaves.

Roll out large rounds of dough. Spread some of the mince mixture on each around the centre, leaving four flaps around circumference. Fold these and seal with egg or water. Roll lightly and even out. Beat eggs with flour and some salt; dip the patties in this, and fry in hot ghee till golden brown, on griddle.

BAINGAN MASALA

1 large brinjal (cut into 6 slices)	1 tbsp. coriander/cummin powder
¼ cup semolina	½ tsp. turmeric
Salt	3-4 tbsp. oil
	Some chopped coriander

Grind 5 green chillies, 5 cloves garlic, ½ bunch coriander leaves, ¼ coconut, walnut size balls of tamarind and jaggery.

Mix the turmeric and coriander/cummin powder with the ground spices along with salt. Apply this to the brinjal slices and marinate for one hour. Dip the slices into semolina, and coat well on both sides. Heat oil in a frying pan, fry the brinjal on both sides till done. Place in serving dish. If any masala is left over, fry in same oil, and spread over brinjals. Sprinkle coriander leaves on top whilst serving.

SUKI DHAL

- ½ kg. urad dhal
- ½ cup oil or ghee
- Salt
- 1 cup beaten curds
- 1 small bunch cut coriander leaves
- 8 cut green chillies
- 1" finely cut ginger
- 1½ tsp. garam masala powder
- Lime juice to taste

Mix chillies, ginger and garam masala together, and mix the dhal in these. In an earthenware pot put some ghee, arrange dhal mixture on top and half the curds—repeat these layers. Line pot with dough, and seal with a lid. Place on a slow fire (preferably charcoal). When hot, put a weight on the lid (to prevent steam escaping) and reduce heat. Cook for 20 more minutes. Remove from fire, but keep pan sealed for an hour. This dhal will keep well for 4-5 days. Sprinkle lime and coriander leaves whilst serving.

NAAN CHAAP

- 1 kg. coarsely minced meat
- ¼ kg. meat fat
- ¼ cup ghee
- 4 whole green chillies
- 1 tsp. garam masala powder
- 1 tsp. ground ginger
- 1 tsp. ground garlic
- Some cut mint and coriander leaves

Grind dry after roasting 6 red chillies, 2 tbsp. coriander, 2 tsp. aniseed, 1 tbsp. poppy seeds.

Boil mince dry with salt. Heat ghee, fry all the

spices, add mince and fat and cook over a slow fire till soft. Add salt, mint and coriander.

Serve with naans.

APPLE CHUTNEY

- 1½ kg. peeled and cut green apples
- 4 cups brown sugar
- 6 cups vinegar
- ¼ kg. sultanas
- ¼ kg. raisins
- Salt
- 3 tbsp. oil
- 3 large chopped onions
- 1 whole pod garlic (crushed coarsely)
- 20 cut green chillies
- 2" piece ginger (cut into fine strips)
- 1 tbsp. mustard seeds
- 20 curry leaves

Heat oil, add mustard seeds. When they start crackling, fry curry leaves, onions, ginger, garlic and green chillies till onions are light brown. Add sugar and vinegar and bring to the boil. Add apples, raisins, sultanas and salt. Simmer till apples are pulpy and the consistency slightly thick. Cool and bottle.

SHREDDED CHICKEN VINDALOO

- 2 cups raw shredded chicken
- 1 sliced onion
- 1 large cut tomato
- 3 tbsp. ghee
- 1 tsp. sugar
- ½ tsp. salt
- ¼ kg. boiled and cut potatoes (optional)

Grind in vinegar, 1 tsp. mustard seeds, 1 tsp. cummin seeds, ½ tsp. turmeric, 12 cloves garlic, 1" ginger, 15 red chillies (seeds removed).

Heat ghee, fry onions till light in colour. Fry the chicken and ground spices; add tomatoes and ½ cup water, salt and sugar. Cook till chicken is tender. Mix in the potatoes.

KOLMI SIRKA ACHAR

1 kg. cleaned prawns
1 kg. oil
750 ml. vinegar
Salt

3 large minced onions
12 curry leaves

Grind to a paste with vinegar 25 red chillies, 2 whole pods garlic, 1 tbsp. peppercorns.

Heat oil, fry curry leaves till crisp, add onions and fry till brown. Add ground spices and prawns, and fry well, adding vinegar a little at a time. Add salt. Simmer for 5 minutes. When cool, store in a dry jar. Keep only for 4-6 weeks.

MACHALI-ACHAR PUNJABI

1 large pomfret
1 tbsp. sugar
¼ tbsp. salt
¾ kg. oil

2 green chillies, chopped
6 cloves garlic, chopped
8 curry leaves

Grind to a paste in vinegar, 4 red chillies, 2 green chillies, ½ tsp. turmeric, 8 cloves garlic, ½" ginger, 6 curry leaves, ½ tsp. cummin seeds, 2 tsp. coriander seeds, ½ tsp. mustard seeds, ½ tsp. fenugreek.

Cut the fish into pieces and fry till crisp. In heated oil, fry the chillies, garlic and curry leaves. When light brown add spice paste and fry well. Add sugar and salt, then put in fish and remove from fire. Cool and bottle.

POMFRET PICKLE

2 large pomfrets	8 green chillies
2 cups oil	2 cups vinegar
12 curry leaves	2 tbsp. sugar
1 tbsp. mustard and cummin seeds mixed	
Salt	
1 tsp. aniseed	

Grind 3 tbsp. chilli powder, 2 tbsp. poppy seeds, 1 whole pod garlic, 1" ginger, ½ tsp. turmeric.

Cut the pomfret into pieces and fry in oil till well browned. Heat oil, fry curry leaves, aniseed, mustard and cummin seeds. Then add green chillies. Add ground spices and fry, adding vinegar, a little at a time. Add sugar and fried fish, mix well and boil once before removing from heat. Store in dry, wide jars.

KOLMI NARIEL PULAO

2 cups cleaned prawns
2 cups washed rice
Salt
2 sliced hard-boiled eggs
4 potatoes (cut into finger chips and fried)
½ cup ghee

Milk of 1 coconut
1 bay leaf
1 tsp. whole garam masala
2 cut large tomatoes

Grind ½ coconut, 1 onion, 10 red chillies, 6 cloves garlic, salt, ½ tsp. turmeric, 1 tbsp. coriander, 1 tsp. cummin seeds, 1 tsp. aniseed.

Heat 2 tbsp ghee and fry ground paste. Add prawns and tomatoes and ½ cup water, and cook till prawns are done. Keep aside. In remaining ghee, fry bay leaf and whole spices; then fry rice, add salt and coconut milk. When rice is nearly done, stir in the potatoes. Spread the prawn masala on top and keep on a low fire for 15 minutes. Arrange egg slices on top whilst serving.

PRAWN PATIA

3 cups shelled prawns
Milk of 1 coconut
2 large minced onions
4 large cut tomatoes
Salt
3 peeled and cut potatoes
¼ cup thick tamarind water
½ cup oil

4 drumsticks (cut into pieces and boiled)
Handful cut coriander leaves

Grind to a paste 15 red chillies, ½ tsp. turmeric, 10 cloves garlic, ¼ dry coconut, 1 tbsp. coriander seeds, 1 tsp. cummin seeds, salt.

Heat oil, fry onions till pinkish, put in paste and fry well. Add prawns, potatoes and tomatoes and fry together till prawns turn pinkish orange in colour. Then add coconut milk, and cook till a thick gravy is formed. Add drumsticks and tamarind water; cook for 5 minutes, then remove from fire. Garnish with chopped coriander leaves.

Serve with kitchri.

GOAN MASALA POMFRET

1 large, cleaned whole pomfret

Oil to fry

Grind (in vinegar) 15 red chillies (seeds removed), 6 cloves garlic, 1 tsp. cummin seeds, salt, 1 tsp. sugar, ½ medium onion, 6 peppercorns, 1 small ball of tamarind (size of a walnut).

Cook the ground spices for 3 minutes over a medium fire in a small saucepan (no ghee to be added), stuff into centre of fish, and apply all over. Heat oil and fry the whole pomfret till well browned on both sides. Do not turn for 5 minutes. Serve with bread, or plain with salad.

HARA MASALA ALOO

½ kg. peeled, boiled and cut potatoes
Salt
Juice of 2 lemons
2 tbsp. oil

1 tbsp. cut coriander leaves
6 curry leaves
4 cloves garlic crushed
½ tsp. mustard seeds
½ tsp. cummin seeds

Grind 6 green chillies, 6 cloves garlic, ¼ bunch coriander leaves, ½ tsp. cummin seeds.

Heat oil and fry curry leaves, garlic, mustard and cummin seeds. Then fry ground spices for 2 minutes, add potatoes and salt and fry till well mixed. Lastly add lemon juice. Sprinkle coriander on top whilst serving. Serve with purees.

LAL MASALA ALOO

½ kg. small boiled and peeled potatoes
Salt
2 tbsp. oil

½ cup imli water
1 tbsp. cut coriander
6 curry leaves
½ tsp. mustard seed

Grind 6 red chillies, ½ tsp. cummin seeds, 6 cloves garlic, ¼ tsp. turmeric.

Heat oil and fry curry leaves and mustard seeds. Then add the ground spices and fry for 2 minutes. Put in potatoes, and when well mixed with the spices, add salt, imli and coriander leaves. Stir till well mixed. Serve with purees.

MOONG RAGDA

- ¼ kg. moong (soaked overnight)
- Salt
- ½ cup thick tamarind water
- 1 tsp. jaggery
- 1 small bunch spring onions, chopped
- 2 tbsp. chopped mint
- 2 tbsp. chopped coriander
- 1 tsp. powdered garam masala
- 1 stick cinnamon
- 2 cloves
- 4 peppercorns
- 2 cardamoms
- 3 tbsp. oil
- 1 large sliced onion

Grind 6 cloves crushed garlic, ¼ tsp. turmeric, 1 tsp. chilli powder, 1 tsp. coriander seed powder, ½ tsp. cummin seed powder.

Heat oil and fry the sliced onion till brown; add the ground spices and salt. Put in moong and fry for 3-4 minutes. Add 4 cups hot water and cook covered till tender. Add chopped spring onions with leaves, coriander, mint and tamarind water mixed with jaggery. Cook for 10 minutes on a low fire. Serve with garam masala powder sprinkled on top.

LIVER MASALA

- 1 liver cleaned and cut into fingers
- ¼ cup oil
- 1 large sliced onion
- 1 tsp. sugar
- Salt
- 2 large potatoes peeled and cut into fingers
- 8 curry leaves

Grind (in vinegar) 8 red chillies, ½" ginger, 8 cloves garlic, 2 tsp. coriander/cummin powder, ¼ tsp. turmeric, handful of coriander, ¼ fresh coconut.

Heat oil, fry curry leaves, then brown onion well. Add ground spices and fry till oil rises to the top. Add liver and stir well for 2-3 minutes. Add 4 cups hot water and simmer with lid on, till liver is cooked. Add salt, potatoes and sugar, and cook gently till potatoes are done. Serve with bread or boiled rice.

RAW MANGO PRESERVE

1 kg. raw mangoes	¼ kg. oil
10 whole green chillies	Salt

Grind 1 medium size bunch coriander leaves, salt, 1 whole pod garlic, 6 tbsp. curry powder.

Wipe the mangoes with a wet cloth and cut into slices. Heat oil well and fry the mango slices till the skin is light brown: remove. In same oil fry the chillies and ground spices for 5 minutes. Put in the mango slices and stir once. Remove from heat. Keep in a dry glass or china bowl in a cool place. This will keep for 8-10 days.

TOMATO CHUTNEY

1½ kg. chopped tomatoes
½ kg. coarsely pounded
   jaggery
¼ kg. sugar

Salt
¼ cup mustard oil
550 ml. vinegar
20 curry leaves

Grind 18 red chillies, 2" ginger, 2 whole pods garlic, 1 tbsp. cummin seeds, 2 tbsp. mustard seeds, ½ tsp. turmeric powder.

Heat oil, fry curry leaves; add the ground spices and fry well. Add the tomatoes, and fry for 5 minutes. Add salt, sugar, jaggery and vinegar. Bring to the boil; then cook on a low fire till slightly thick and sticky. Cool and bottle.

SÁBZI ACHAR

¼ kg. peas (shelled)
¼ kg. cauliflower cut into
   sprigs
¼ kg. turnips peeled and cut
1 tbsp. salt

¼ kg. peeled and cut
   carrots
2 cups vinegar
¼ kg jaggery (coarsely
   powdered)

Grind 10 red chillies, 1 pod garlic, 2" ginger, 2 tbsp. mustard seeds.

Parboil all the vegetables and strain and cool them. In a pan put the vinegar and jaggery, and bring to the boil. Add salt and ground spices and fry well for 2-3 minutes. Add vegetables, mix well, and remove from the fire. Cool and bottle.

KIDNEYS ON TOAST

- 9 large kidneys (cut finely)
- 2 large tomatoes, minced
- 2 onions, minced
- 2 tbsp. ghee
- 1 cup water
- 1" ginger
- 4 cloves garlic ground together
- 1 tsp. chilli powder
- 1 tbsp. curry powder
- 2 tbsp. Worcestershire sauce
- ¼ bunch coriander leaves
- Salt
- 10 slices bread, halved and fried

Fry onions in hot ghee till brown; then add ground ginger, garlic, curry and chilli powders. Fry for a minute, then add kidneys, tomatoes and coriander leaves. Add 1 cup water and cook gently till the water dries and kidneys are ready. Add sauce and salt and pile onto fried bread. Garnish with coriander leaves.

KIDNEYS AND CHOPS MASALA

- ¼ kg. mutton chops
- 2 kidneys, cut into 8 pieces
- ½ tsp. ground garlic
- ½ tsp. ground ginger
- 2 tbsp. ghee
- Salt
- Juice of 1 lemon
- 1 minced onion

Grind 4 green chillies, ½ bunch coriander leaves, 4 cloves garlic, 1 tsp. poppy seeds, 1 tsp aniseed, 1 tsp. garam masala, 1 tsp. curry powder.

Boil the chops and kidneys with ginger and garlic Heat ghee and fry onion till brown. Add ground spices and fry well. Put in the chops and kidneys and fry for a few minutes longer. Add lemon juice, take off from fire.

MASALA BAKED POMFRET

1 large pomfret (boiled & flaked)
½ ltr. milk
Salt and pepper to taste

3 tbsp. flour
2-3 tbsp. ghee

To be cut finely: 1 medium onion, 4 green chillies, ½ inch piece of ginger, ¼ bunch mint leaves, ½ bunch coriander leaves.

Heat the ghee, fry the onion, ginger and green chillies till the onion is light brown. Mix the milk and flour to a smooth paste, pour into the onions and stir till thick. Then add salt, pepper, flaked fish, mint and coriander leaves. Pour into a greased dish and bake in a moderately hot oven (350°F) for 20 minutes.

FISH MASALA ROLLS

8 fish fillets (cut from 2 pomfrets)
2 tbsp. oil
Grind in vinegar 10 dry chillies
Salt
¼ onion
¼ dry coconut

1 tsp. cummin seeds
6 cloves garlic
1 tbsp. jaggery
1 walnut size ball of tamarind

Garnish: 2 sliced tomatoes, ½ cup boiled peas, 2 hard-boiled sliced eggs, ½ kg. mashed potatoes or potato chips.

Fry ground spices well in oil. When cool spread over the fillets; roll them up, tie with a string and place in a greased dish. Bake in a moderately hot oven (350°F) for 20 minutes. Remove the strings. Garnish with mashed or fried potatoes, tomato rings, green peas and egg slices.

MASALA SPAGHETTI

125 gm. boiled spaghetti
2 bunches minced spring onions with leaves
2 tbsp. ghee
Salt
2 eggs
375 gm. minced tomatoes

1 bunch cut celery
½ cup boiled peas
½ bunch cut coriander leaves
½ tsp. mustard seeds
½ tsp. cummin seeds

Grind 1 tsp. curry powder, 6 cloves garlic, 4 peppercorns, 2 cloves, 1 stick cinnamon, ¼ tsp. turmeric powder.

Heat ghee and brown the mustard and cummin seeds. Add ground spices and fry well. Add tomatoes and salt; when tomatoes are soft add the spaghetti, celery and onions. Mix well, then add beaten eggs. Cover and keep on a low fire for 10 minutes. Serve with coriander sprinkled on top and peas all around.

CHANNA BATATA

- 1 cup brown channa
- ¼ kg. peeled, boiled and cut potatoes
- Salt
- ¼ cup thick imli water
- 1 tbsp. jaggery
- 1 tbsp. chopped coriander
- 1 tbsp. chopped mint
- 3 tbsp. oil
- 2 bay leaves

Grind 4 red chillies, 4 green chillies, 1 tsp. cummin seeds, 1/8 dry coconut, 8 cloves garlic, ¼" ginger, ¼ bunch coriander.

Soak channa overnight with ¼ tsp. soda; boil in the same water till tender. Heat oil, put in bay leaves and then fry ground spices well. Add salt, and channa with its liquid. Bring to the boil, simmer for 10 minutes and add potatoes, jaggery, imli, coriander and mint. Simmer for 5 minutes. To be served as a snack.

DAHI BATATA

- ½ kg. boiled and peeled potatoes
- ½ kg. beaten curds
- Salt
- 1 tsp. roasted and pounded cummin seeds
- 2 tbsp. boiled and peeled charoli
- 2 tbsp. sultanas or raisins
- 2 finely minced white onions
- Chilli powder to taste

Grind 6 green chillies, salt, 1 tsp. sugar, 4 cloves garlic, ¼" ginger, ¼ bunch coriander leaves.

Mix the ground spices and curds. Keep aside. Mash the potatoes, form into small cutlets and fill the centres with a mixture of onions and raisins. Arrange in a dish, pour curds over the cutlets, sprinkle with cummin powder, chilli powder, salt and charoli. Serve cold.

SEV CHAAT

- ¼ kg. fine, salty besan ki sev
- ¼ kg. boiled, peeled and cut potatoes
- 2 chopped spring onions with the leaves
- 1 tbsp. chopped mint
- 1 tbsp. coriander leaves
- Juice of 1-2 lemons
- Salt
- 2 stalks cut celery
- 1 chopped capsicum
- ½ tsp. chilli powder
- 2 cut green chillies

Mix all the ingredients together and serve at once.

ALOO CHOLLAS

- ¼ kg. boiled, peeled and cut potatoes
- 1 cup channa
- ¼ bunch cut mint leaves
- ¼ bunch cut coriander leaves
- Salt
- ½ tbsp. chilli powder
- ½ tsp. garam masala powder
- 1 tsp. roasted and powdered cummin seeds
- 1 cup thick imli water
- 1 sliced onion
- 1 walnut size lump jaggery

Grind ¼ bunch mint, ¼ bunch coriander, 2 green chillies, 1 red chilli, 4 cloves garlic.

Soak channa overnight with ¼ tsp. soda; boil in the same water till tender. In a pan put channa, potatoes, salt, ground spices, cummin and chilli powders, half the mint and coriander and the jaggery dissolved in imli water. Boil for 10 minutes (add water if needed). Remove from heat. Serve with garam masala powder and remaining mint and coriander sprinkled on top.

KOHLAPURI GURDE

8 large kidneys	Salt
1 medium minced onion	1 tbsp. cut coriander
6 curry leaves	
3 tbsp. oil	

Grind 8 red chillies, 8 cloves garlic, ¼" ginger, 1 tsp. cummin, ¼ tsp. turmeric, ½ tsp. garam masala powder, 1 tbsp. jaggery, 1 small lump of imli, walnut size.

Cut the kidneys into small pieces, apply ground spices and keep for 1-2 hours. Heat oil, fry the curry leaves; then add onions and cook till brown. Add kidneys and 1 cup hot water. Bring to the boil, cook uncovered till kidneys are tender and gravy thick. Mix in salt, and garnish with coriander whilst serving. Serve with mashed potatoes as a side dish or as a tea-time savoury on fried bread.

GUAVA CHHAT

- 6 peeled and cut guavas (seeds removed)
- ¼ kg peeled, boiled and cut potatoes
- Salt
- Juice of 2 lemons
- ½ tsp. sugar
- 4 finely cut green chillies
- 3 spring onions cut with the leaves
- 1 tsp. cut coriander
- 1 tsp cut mint

Mix all the ingredients well together in a bowl, and keep cool for an hour before serving.

MOGHLAI DAHI ALOO

- ½ kg. peeled and cut potatoes
- Salt
- ½ kg beaten curds
- ½ tsp. saffron
- 3 tbsp. oil
- ½ tsp. garam masala powder
- ½ cup chopped walnuts
- 6-8 sliced almonds
- 8 curry leaves
- ½ tsp. cummin seeds
- 4 crushed cloves garlic

Cut finely 1 onion (medium), 6 green chillies, ½" ginger, 6 cloves garlic.

Soak the saffron in 1 tbsp. hot water. Heat oil, and brown the curry leaves, cummin seeds and garlic. Add cut spices and brown them. Add the potatoes and fry for 2-3 minutes. Add curds, cover and cook for 5 minutes. Then uncover and simmer till potatoes are done. Add walnuts, salt, saffron and garam masala. Keep on a low fire for 5 minutes. Garnish with almonds when serving.

ELABORATELY YOURS

KHOWSWEY

½ kg. boiled and shredded meat
1 cup meat stock
5 tbsp. ghee
1 large cut onion
1 large cut tomato
Salt

Milk of 1 coconut
2 tbsp. roasted gram flour
¼ kg. spaghetti (boiled)
Garnishes given below

Grind 6 cloves garlic, 1" ginger, 1 tbsp. curry powder, ¼ tsp. turmeric, ½ tsp. chilli powder, salt.

Heat 2 tbsp. ghee, fry onion till brown and add ground spices. Fry well. Add tomato and salt and fry. Then add stock and meat. Simmer for 10 minutes.

Heat 3 tbsp. ghee, fry gram flour, then add coconut milk off the fire. Stir well, return to heat and cook till boiling. Add spaghetti and simmer for 10 minutes. Add salt.

Garnishes (to be kept on table in separate bowls): chopped garlic, chopped ginger, chopped green chillies, cut spring onions, cut mint, cut coriander leaves, finely cut and fried potatoes, 4 red chillies to be fried crisp in oil and then pounded, 2 chopped hard-boiled eggs.

For each helping serve some spaghetti and sauce in bowl, add some meat with its gravy and a little of each of the garnishes.

LAGANIA SHEEKH

½ kg. boiled mince
5 eggs
Salt
Birista of 2 medium onions
3 cut spring onions
3 tbs. gram-dal, boiled and mashed
Handful chopped mint and coriander leaves
2 tbsp. ghee
Juice of 1 lemon

Grind 6 cloves garlic, 4 green chillies, ½" ginger.

Heat ghee, fry ground spices, add mince and salt and fry for 2-3 minutes. Remove from fire, mix mince with dal, spring onions, mint and coriander, birista and 2 eggs. Pour into a greased baking dish. Beat 3 eggs till frothy, spread over mince, and bake at 350°F for half an hour. Cut into diamond shapes and serve with sprinkling of lemon juice.

MASALA JINGA PULAO

2 cups shelled prawns
2 cups rice
1 cup boiled peas
½ cup ghee
½ cup oil
Salt
8 curry leaves
Milk of 1 coconut
2 medium minced onions
Juice of 1 lemon

Grind 15 red chillies, 1 tbsp. coriander seeds, 1 tsp. cummin seeds, ½ tsp. turmeric, salt, 8 cloves garlic, ½ coconut.

Heat oil and fry curry leaves and onions till golden brown. Add ground spices and fry for 3-4 minutes. Add prawns and peas. Cook till the prawns are done, remove from heat and stir in lemon juice.

Heat ghee, fry rice, well and add coconut milk. Cook till nearly done. Spread prawn mixture on top; cover, and cook for 10 minutes on a slow fire.

KITCHRA

1½ kg. cut and boiled meat
¼ kg. ghee
Salt
Birista of ¼ kg. onions
¼ bunch cut mint
¼ bunch coriander leaves
¼ cup rice
¼ cup masoor dhal
¼ cup toover dhal
¼ cup moong dhal
¼ cup channa dhal
2½ cups wheat
1 tsp. garam masala powder
½ cup oil

Grind 12 red chillies, ½ tsp. turmeric, 12 cloves garlic, 1" ginger, 1 tsp. salt.

Soak the wheat overnight in water, strain and pound it the next day to remove husks. Boil all the dhals together till soft. Pass through sieve to get soft consistency and keep aside. Boil rice till soft. Cook wheat with oil and water till very soft. Mix wheat, rice and dhals together. Heat 200 gm. ghee and fry the ground spices well. Add meat and fry for 5 minutes, add meat stock if any. Add wheat etc. and stir well. Mix in birista, salt (if needed), mint, and coriander and simmer for 10 minutes. Sprinkle garam masala on top. Heat 50 gm. ghee, pour sizzling over contents of pan and cover quickly with lid. Simmer covered for 15 minutes.

Serve with tandur ki roti, lemon, chilli powder, whole mint leaves and white onion slices.

MOOTHIYAS

- ¾ kg. meat
- 1 tsp. ground garlic
- 1 tsp. ground ginger
- 2 cups stock
- 3 tbsp. ghee
- 2 tbsp. curry powder
- ¼ tsp. turmeric
- Salt
- 1 cut tomato (large)
- ½ grated coconut
- 2 chopped onions
- 2 peeled and cut potatoes
- 125 gm. chopped cluster beans
- 1 bunch chopped spinach
- 1 bunch chopped chawli bhaji
- 1 bunch chopped khatti bhaji
- 125 gm. boiled dry beans (val)
- 3 cut and boiled drumsticks
- 1 tsp. garam masala powder

Grind ½ bunch coriander, 6 red chillies, 2 green chillies, 6 cloves garlic, 1 tsp. cummin, 1 tbsp. coriander.

Boil the meat with ginger and garlic. Brown onions in hot ghee. Add the ground spices, turmeric and curry powder and fry well. Add stock, potatoes, cluster beans, the leafy vegetables, and salt. Cover and cook till potatoes are nearly done. Add meat, tomato, coconut, and val. Then drop in the moothiyas, simmer with lid on for 5-10 minutes. Sprinkle garam masala on top.

Moothiyas: 1 cup bajri flour, 2 tbsp. ghee, salt ½ grated coconut, 1 tbsp curry powder, 3 bunches chopped fenugreek leaves.

Mix all the ingredients well and add sufficient water to make a dough. Form into moothiyas (elongated dumplings)

KAJU CHICKEN

1 chicken, cut and boiled
1 cup chicken stock
2 minced onions
2 tbsp. ghee
125 gm. ground cashewnuts

1 tsp. mixed whole spices
(cardamom, cloves, peppercorns)
¼ kg. curds, beaten

Grind ½ bunch coriander leaves, 8 green chillies, 1″ ginger, 7 cloves garlic.

Fry onions in hot ghee till soft. Add ground ingredients and garam masala and fry well. Add stock gradually, then put in the beaten curds. Boil for a few minutes, then add the chicken. Simmer for a few minutes. Add ground cashewnuts and boil once before removing from fire.

PULAO IN LAYERS

3 cups cooked rice   1 hard-boiled egg

Green Layer:

Grind ½ coconut, 1 tsp. cummin seeds, 4 cloves garlic, 4 green chillies, ½ tsp. sugar, ½ tsp. salt, ¼ bunch mint leaves, ½ bunch coriander leaves, juice of 1 lemon.

Red Layer:

2 tbsp. ghee
2 grated onions   1 large ground tomato

Grind 8 cloves garlic, 6 red chillies, ½" ginger, salt, ½ tsp. garam masala powder.

Yellow Layer:

½ tsp. powdered saffron   2 tbsp. lemon juice

Mix 1 cup cooked rice with green ground spices and spread in a greased mould.

In ghee, fry onions till light brown; add red ground spices. Fry well. Add tomato, and when boiling, mix 1 cup rice. Remove from fire and press into mould over green layer.

Mix saffron, lemon juice and remaining rice. Press into mould. Heat for 10 minutes, then turn out on a plate. Decorate with coriander leaves and a sliced hard-boiled egg.

KASHMIRI GOSHT

1 kg. cut meat
½ kg. beaten curds
½ kg. grated onions
¼ cup ghee
Salt
2 tbsp. chilli powder

3 tbsp. ground poppy seeds
½ cup ground walnuts
½ tsp. heated and powdered saffron
1 tbsp. milk

Marinate the meat for 4-5 hours in curds with ghee, salt, and onions. Mix the saffron with milk. Cook the meat till soft, then add all the remaining ingredients and fry to a reddish brown colour. Serve with parathas.

MUTTON KOHANI

- 1 kg. cubed meat
- ¼ ltr. milk
- 6 tbsp. ghee
- ¼ kg. cut tomatoes
- 2 ground onions
- 8 cloves garlic
- 1" ginger, ground
- Salt
- 1 tsp. garam masala powder
- 1 tsp. chilli powder

Boil the meat in milk, adding 2 tbsp. ghee. When the milk has thickened and the meat is nearly tender, add onions, garlic, ginger and tomatoes. Fry well, adding ghee as it sticks to pan. When meat is tender, add salt, chilli powder and garam masala. Serve with hot parathas.

MUTTON AND CORN PULAO

- 1 tin whole corn kernels
- or
- 2 cups fresh corn kernels (well boiled)
- 3 cups cooked rice
- 2 minced onions
- 3 tbsp. ghee
- ½ kg. meat (cubed and boiled with salt)
- 1 cup meat stock
- Salt

Grind ½ bunch coriander leaves, 8 green chillies, 8 cloves garlic, 1" ginger, 1 tbsp. curry powder.

Heat ghee, fry onions till light brown. Fry ground spices, add stock, then add meat, salt and corn. Spread over warm rice.

CHICKEN CURRY

1 cut and boiled chicken
2 cups chicken stock
2½ cups thick milk from large coconut
¼ cup thick tamarind water
8 curry leaves
½ tsp salt
6 tbsp. ghee
½ bunch coriander leaves chopped
1 tsp. garam masala powder

Roast and then grind: 10 red chillies, 1 large onion, ¼ dry coconut, 2 tbsp. poppy seeds, 15 cashewnuts, 2 tbsp. coriander seeds, ½ tsp. turmeric powder, 10 cloves garlic, 1 tbsp. sesame seeds, 2 tbsp. peanuts, 2 tbsp. channas, ½" piece ginger.

Heat 4 tbsp. ghee, fry curry leaves, then the ground ingredients. When well fried, add stock gradually; then add coconut milk, salt and coriander leaves and cook till thick. Next add the chicken and tamarind water and cook till boiling. Heat remaining 2 tbsp. ghee. Sprinkle garam masala on curry, then pour hot ghee on top and quickly cover. Serve after 5 minutes. Serve with boiled rice or bread.

NARGISI KOFTA KORMA

½ kg. mince meat
¼ tsp. ground ginger
¼ tsp. ground garlic
Salt
4 cloves
3 cardamoms
6 peppercorns
½" cinnamon
6 hard-boiled eggs, halved
1 cup beaten curds
¼ tsp. ground saffron
1 tbsp. ground channas
1 egg
Few sliced almonds
Ghee

Grind 6 red chillies, 1 large onion, ½ tbsp. turmeric, 6 cloves garlic, ½" ginger, 1 tbsp. coriander seeds, 1 tsp. poppy seeds.

Boil the mince with salt, ginger, garlic, cloves, cardamoms, peppercorns and cinnamon; then grind it to a smooth consistency. Mix mince with channa and egg. Cover egg halves with mince and fry in ghee till brown; keep aside.

Heat 4 tbsp. ghee and fry ground spices well. Add the curds and simmer gently till well mixed. Add saffron, stir once, and gently add the koftas (mince balls). Cook for 2-3 minutes. Do not stir, only shake pan from side to side. Sprinkle almonds on top before serving. Serve with naan or a plain pulao.

MUGHLAI MURGH MASALA

1 cleaned and cut chicken
1 cup beaten curds
Salt
9 large sliced onions
6 tbsp. ghee
1 tsp. caraway seed
4 cloves
4 cardamoms
½ tsp. peppercorns
1 stick cinnamon

Grind 8 red chillies, 2 green chillies, ½ tbsp. turmeric, 1 tbsp. coriander, 8 cloves garlic, ½" ginger, 1 medium size onion.

In hot ghee, brown the onions and whole spices. Remove from ghee, grind together and mix with curds. In the same ghee fry ground spices well; add chicken and fry till chicken is brown. Add two cups water, and salt. Cover and cook till chicken is nearly done. Add the curd mixture and cook uncovered till chicken is tender and gravy thick.

Serve with naan or parathas.

AJMERI CURRY

½ kg meat (boiled)
Milk of 1 coconut
2 tbsp. ghee
6 curry leaves
½ cup thick tamarind water (or juice of 2 lemons)
1 tsp. salt
1 tsp. garam masala powder
¼ kg. boiled, peeled potatoes
Few cut coriander leaves

Grind 8 cloves garlic, ½" ginger, 10 red chillies, ¼ dry coconut (or 2 tbsp. dessicated coconut), 3 tbsp. peanuts, 3 tbsp. gram, 2 tbsp. coriander seeds, ½ tbsp. cummin seeds, 1 tbsp. poppy seeds, 8 almonds, 1 large onion.

Heat ghee; fry the curry leaves, then add ginger, garlic and ground spices. Add meat and salt. When the masala is well fried, add coconut milk and potatoes. Boil for a few minutes, then add coriander leaves, garam masala powder and tamarind water. Boil once before removing from the fire.

PULAO PESHAWARI

1 kg. cut meat
½ kg. rice
¼ kg. sliced onions
¼ kg. ghee
¼ kg. beaten curds
Salt
8 cloves ground garlic

½" ground ginger
½ tsp. saffron
3 tbsp. kewra
Silver foil
Handful sliced and fried almonds

Powder 1 tsp. caraway seeds, ½ tsp. peppercorns, 2" cinnamon, 8 cardamoms, 8 cloves.

Grind the saffron to a paste with kewra. Brown the onions in hot ghee. Remove and crush them to powder; then mix them with spice powder and stir both into beaten curds. In the same ghee, fry meat with ginger, garlic and salt, till well browned. Add 2 cups hot water and cook till tender. Add the curd mixture, rice and 1 cup hot water. Stir well and when rice is nearly cooked, stir in saffron-kewra. Cover pan with wet cloth and put the lid over it. Keep on a slow fire for 15 minutes. Garnish with silver foil and almonds. Serve with onion salad.

KORMA SHAHI

1 cleaned and cut chicken
1 cup beaten curds
Salt
4 tbsp. ghee

½ tsp. saffron
1 tbsp. kewra
3 large sliced onions
25 almonds peeled and ground

Grind 10 red chillies, 1 tbsp. coriander, ½ tsp. turmeric, ½ tsp. salt, 8 cloves garlic, ½" ginger.

Powder 1" cinnamon, 4 cloves, 6 peppercorns, 4 cardamoms.

Grind the saffron to a paste with kewra. Brown onions well in ghee, then add the ground spices and fry. Add chicken and fry well till brown. Add 2 cups hot water and cook covered till chicken is nearly done. Put in curds, powdered spices and almond paste. Simmer for 10 minutes. Add saffron just before removing from heat.

Serve with naan or a plain pulao.

KABABS MOGHLAI

½ kg. mince
1 onion
1 tsp. cummin seed
Salt
8 red chillies
1 tbsp. coriander seeds
3 tbsp. gram dhal
Juice of 1 lemon
Oil or ghee to fry

Pound four 1" sticks of cinnamon, 10 peppercorns, 4 cloves, 2 cardamoms, ½ tsp. grated nutmeg, 4 small sticks of mace.

Grind 3 walnuts, 8 cashewnuts, 1 tbsp. poppy seeds, 10 peeled almonds.

Cut finely 6 green chillies, 1 large onion, ¼ bunch coriander leaves, 1/6th bunch mint leaves.

Boil the mince with onion, cummin, salt, chillies, coriander seeds and dhal, then grind it to a fine paste. Add lemon juice and pounded and ground ingredients.

mix well, and form into kababs, filling the centre with mixed cut ingredients. Fry in very little ghee, till well browned on both sides.

SPINACH MUTTON PULAO

1 kg. boiled meat
2 cups stock
½ kg good rice (par-boiled)
6 tbsp. ghee
Salt
¼ kg. curds
¼ kg. minced onions

Chop 1 bunch each of fenugreek leaves and spinach. Grind 15 green chillies, 10 cloves garlic, ½" ginger, 1 tsp. cummin seeds, ½ tsp. turmeric, 1 stick cinnamon, 6 cloves, 6 cardamoms, 8 peppercorns.

Heat 4 tbsp ghee, fry onions till light brown; add ground spices and fry for 2-3 minutes. Add salt and all the leafy vegetables and fry again for 5 minutes. Put in the meat, stock and beaten curds. Cover and simmer for 10 minutes; then remove cover and cook for 15 minutes longer over a fast fire, till thick gravy is formed. Place rice in a layer on top and pour 2 tbsp. heated ghee over it. Cook on a slow fire for 20 minutes. Serve with an onion salad.

BAKED COCONUT FISH

1 pomfret (filleted)	Salt
1 egg	Juice of 1 lemon
1 stalk cut celery	1 tsp. sugar
½ kg. mashed potatoes	1 tsp. pepper
1 cup milk	1 grated coconut
1 tbsp. butter	1 tsp. cummin seed
2 tbsp. ghee	powder

Chop finely: 2 onions, 5 green chillies, 8 cloves garlic, ¼" ginger, ½ bunch coriander leaves.

Fry the fillets with a little salt. Mix mashed potatoes with milk and butter whilst still warm. Rub all the chopped ingredients, pepper, cummin seed powder, salt, sugar, lemon juice, coconut and celery well together. Heat ghee, and fry this mixture for a few minutes. Lay fish in greased dish, spread fried masala on top, cover with creamed potatoes, spread top with beaten egg and bake at 375°F for 20 minutes.

JALIWALLAY CUTLETS

½ kg. minced meat	8 to 10 eggs
4 slices bread	Salt to taste
½ to 1 cup dry bread-	Ghee for frying
crumbs	

Grind 1" ginger, 8 cloves garlic, 6 green chillies. Soak the bread in water for ½ an hour, then squeeze out the water. Beat 4 eggs at a time with ¼ cup water.

Mix ground spices and mince and keep aside for at least 2 hours. Add soaked bread and salt. Mix well and shape into cutlets. Roll cutlets in breadcrumbs, dip them in egg and fry well on both sides. Sprinkle egg around each cutlet whilst frying, to form a sort of lace frill around it.

HARISA

1½ cups wheat
6 cups water
3 tbsp. oil
1 medium chicken or
 ½ kg. mutton
2 cups milk
Birista of 2 medium onions
Salt
¼ cup ghee

1" ginger cut into strips
Few mint leaves
1 tsp. garam masala
 powder

Grind 3 green chillies, 4 cloves garlic, 1 tsp. salt, ½" ginger.

Boil the chicken or mutton with the ground spices, then flake it. Soak and pound the wheat. Dry in a flat tray and blow off husks. Cook in 6 cups water and oil till soft. Sieve, by mixing milk, a little at a time. Put into a pan with chicken or meat, add 2 tbsp. ghee and cook for 10 minutes, stir to prevent sticking to pan. Remove from heat. Sprinkle garam masala and sliced ginger on top. Pour hot ghee over this. Serve with birista and mint leaves sprinkled on top.

JALI CHICKEN

1 cleaned and cut chicken
Salt
3-4 eggs
1 cup breadcrumbs
Ghee to fry

Grind 6 cloves garlic, 6 red chillies, ½" ginger.

Boil chicken with ground spices and salt in 1½ cups water. Boil till tender, and water dries.

Beat eggs with ¾ cup water. Dip chicken pieces in egg, then in breadcrumbs and fry well, sprinkling some of the egg on top to form a sort of lace frill around each piece. Serve hot.

BIRYANI

2 cups rice (parboiled)
½ kg. mutton (cubed and boiled)
½ kg. peeled and fried potatoes
¼ kg. beaten curds
Salt
200 gm. ghee
Birista of ½ kg. onions
½ tsp. saffron (heated and powdered)
¼ tsp. orange food colouring
3 tbsp. milk

Grind ½" ginger, 8 dry red chillies, 6 cloves garlic, 2 green chillies, ¼ bunch coriander leaves.

Powder 1" cinnamon, 3 cardamoms, 6 cloves, 6 peppercorns.

In beaten curds, mix in ground ingredients, powdered spices, salt, meat, birista of onions, potatoes, and half the melted ghee. Lay rice over this, pour remaining ghee on top. Mix saffron, colouring and milk and sprinkle this over rice. Seal pan with a paste made of wheat flour and water. Cook on a fast fire for 10 minutes till steam begins to escape from sides of pan, then put in a hot oven 400°F for 15-20 minutes. Remove seal just before serving.

MOGHLAI MEAT ROAST

¼ kg. meat (cut and boiled)
½ cup meat stock
3 peeled and fried potatoes
3 hard-boiled eggs
1 cup beaten curds
Birista of ¼ kg. onions
30 gm. cleaned and boiled charoli
3 tbsp. ghee
Salt
1 tsp. whole garam masala
¼ tsp. saffron (heated and powdered)

Grind 10 red chillies, ½ tsp. turmeric, 3 green chillies, 8 cloves garlic, 1" ginger.

Heat ghee, fry the whole spices; add ground spices and fry well. Then add stock and meat, birista of onions, salt, curds and saffron. When gravy is thick add potatoes. Remove from fire and put into a dish with the eggs. Sprinkle charoli on top.

PRAWN BIRYANI

- 2 cups shelled prawns
- 3 cups rice (to be parboiled)
- Salt
- ¼ kg. ghee
- 3 minced onions
- 3 bay leaves
- 3 peeled and cubed potatoes
- 4 large cut tomatoes
- 1 tbsp. powdered garam masala
- ¼ tsp. saffron (heated and powdered)
- Some cut mint and coriander leaves
- ¼ kg. beaten curds
- ½ tsp. yellow colour (mixed in 3 tbsp. water)

Grind 12 red chillies, 2 tbsp. dhania, ½ tsp. turmeric, 1 tsp. cummin seeds, salt, 8 cloves garlic, ½" ginger.

In half the ghee, fry bay leaves and brown onions. Add the ground spices and when well fried, add potatoes and prawns and fry them. Add the tomatoes and cook on a slow fire till the potatoes are cooked. Remove pan from heat, mix in curds, saffron, garam masala, mint and coriander and stir. Arrange rice on top, pour remaining ghee (melted) over it, sprinkle with yellow colour, cover with a lid, and keep first on a fast fire for 5-7 minutes and then on a slow fire for 15 minutes.

ZAFFRANI KORMA

- ½ kg. mutton cut into small pieces
- 12 kidneys halved
- 1¼ cups beaten curds
- 2 large sliced onions
- Salt
- 6 whole green chillies (slit in the centre)
- 3 tbsp. ghee
- ¼ tsp. saffron
- ½" ginger (cut into strips)
- 8 cloves garlic (cut into strips)
- 1 stick cinnamon
- 4 cloves
- 6 peppercorns
- 4 cardamoms

Soak the saffron in 1 tsp. water, then grind it. Heat ghee, fry whole spices, chillies, ginger and garlic. Add meat and onions and fry till light brown. Add kidneys and salt, and cook uncovered till meat is tender and gravy slightly thick. Mix saffron into curds and add these to the meat, off the fire. Bring to boil and serve with parathas.

MURGH MUSSALAM

- 1 whole cleaned chicken
- ¾ cup beaten curds
- 2 bay leaves
- 1 whole hard-boiled egg
- Salt
- 2 tbsp. fried sultanas
- 10 almonds peeled, sliced and fried
- 1 large sliced onion
- ½ tsp. peppercorns
- 2 tsp. kewra
- ¼ tsp. ground saffron
- 2 cardamoms
- 1 stick cinnamon
- 3 cloves
- Ghee

Grind 1 large onion, 10 cloves garlic, ½" ginger, 1 tbsp. coriander powder, 1 tsp. chilli powder.

Brown the sliced onion in ghee and grind it with the peppercorns. In 4 tbsp. ghee, brown the whole spices and bay leaves. Add ground spices and fry well. Remove from fire. Take 1 tbsp. of mixture from pan and mix with the whole egg, salt, sultanas and almonds. Fill this into the centre of chicken and tie up the chicken.

Put pan of fried spices on the fire again and add the chicken, curds, browned onion, salt and 3 cups of hot water. Cook on medium heat till chicken is nearly tender. Then increase the heat and cook till the water dries. When the masala begins to coat sides of chicken, remove from heat and add the kewra and saffron. Serve with silver foil. To be eaten with parathas.

PASANDE PESHAWARI

1¼ kg. leg of mutton
2 cups beaten curds
1 tsp. ground ginger
1 tsp. ground garlic
3 tbsp. ghee
3 large sliced onions

Salt
2 sliced hard-boiled eggs

Powder 1 stick cinnamon, 4 cloves, 6 peppercorns, 4 cardamoms.

Grind 2 tbsp. poppy seeds, 20 peeled almonds, ¼ tsp. saffron, 1 tbsp. coriander seeds, 8 red chillies, ¼ tsp. turmeric.

Cut the meat into thin slices and beat these till they are thin and flat. Marinate the meat slices in a mixture of 1 cup curds, ginger, garlic and ½ tsp. salt for 1 hour. Heat ghee, fry onions till well browned, remove and crush to a fine powder. In the same ghee, put meat and ground coriander seeds, chillies and turmeric. Cover and cook over a slow fire till meat is tender and gravy dry. Add fried onions, the remaining curds, salt, if needed, and ground poppy seeds, almonds and saffron. Cook uncovered till gravy is thick; stir quite frequently. Sprinkle powdered spices on top, and garnish with egg slices. Serve with parathas.

MURGH JEHANGIRI

1 whole cleaned chicken
3-4 tbsp. ghee
3 bay leaves
Salt
¼ tsp. ground saffron

2 medium ground onions
2 cups beaten curds

Grind: ½" ginger, 8 cloves garlic, 4 green chillies, 3 cloves, 1" cinnamon, 3 cardamoms, 1 tsp. aniseed.

Prick the chicken well with a fork. Mix curds with ground spices and rub over chicken. Set aside the chicken to marinate for 3-4 hours. Heat ghee, fry bay leaves, brown onions well, then add the chicken with the marinade. Cook on medium heat till nearly done. Add salt and saffron, and fry chicken till the masala begins to coat chicken and it is well browned. Serve whole, with silver foil on top.

For added richness, 2 chopped hard-boiled eggs,

some fried sliced almonds and fried sultanas may be sprinkled on top.

Serve with fried rice, naan or parathas.

MUGHLAI PULAO NURJEHANI

1 cleaned and cut chicken	Handful sliced and fried almonds
1 kg minced meat	
8 tbsp. ghee	3 bay leaves
4 large minced onions	2" cinnamon
¼ kg. curds	12 cloves
¾ kg. rice	12 cardamoms
Salt	18 peppercorns
¼ tsp. ground saffron	

Grind 1 pod garlic, ¾" ginger, 2 tsp. chilli powder, 2 tsp. coriander/cummin powder, ½ tsp. turmeric.

In 4 tbsp. ghee, fry 2 onions, till brown. Add half the whole spices, then put in the chicken and mince, and brown. Add ground spices and fry for a few minutes along with chicken and mince. Add 2 cups hot water, cover and cook till chicken is tender. Beat curds with saffron and add to chicken. Cook uncovered for 10 minutes. Remove from fire and keep aside.

Heat the remaining ghee, fry the bay leaves and remaining whole spices. Add the onions and brown them well. Add rice, and fry till brown. Add enough water to cook rice (add 1 tsp. salt). Spread a layer of rice on a flat serving dish, then a layer of meat; repeat with one more layer of each. Garnish with almonds.

MOGHLAI PULAO NARGISI

- ½ kg. boiled chops
- ½ kg. boiled meat
- Salt
- ¼ kg. ghee
- 8 hard-boiled eggs
- ½ kg. onions (sliced and fried)
- A handful of sultanas
- Sliced almonds, fried
- 2 bay leaves
- 2 cups beaten curds
- 1 tbsp whole garam masala
- 1 tsp. ground garlic
- 1 tsp. ground ginger
- ½ kg. parboiled rice
- ½ tsp. saffron
- ½ cup milk

Heat ghee, fry eggs brown and remove. Put in bay leaves; when brown, drain off half the ghee and keep aside. In heated ghee, add ginger and garlic and fry meat and chops till well browned. Remove from heat, add the curds, salt, pepper, garam masala, onions, eggs, sultanas and almonds. Stir well. Arrange the parboiled rice on top, pour heated ghee over the rice, and sprinkle with saffron milk. Cover edges of pan with a paste of flour and water, and put over medium heat for 20 minutes.

PAAYAS

- 9 trotters (cleaned)
- 1 tsp. ground ginger
- 1 tsp. ground garlic
- 1 tsp. whole garam masala
- 2 large ground tomatoes
- 6 cloves crushed garlic
- Birista of 4 large onions
- 2 tbsp. gram flour
- 2 tbsp. oil
- Some cut mint and coriander leaves
- 1 tsp. powdered garam masala
- Ghee

Powder 2 tsp. chilli powder, ½ tsp. turmeric, 2 tsp. coriander/cummin powder.

Boil the trotters with ground ginger and garlic. Heat oil and 2 tbsp. ghee, fry crushed garlic and whole garam masala. Add powdered spices and salt and fry. Then add gram flour. Fry for 2 minutes, add tomatoes, then the trotters. Add the onion birista and cook for 5 minutes. Add mint and coriander leaves and sprinkle garam masala powder on top. Pour 2 tbsp. hot ghee over contents in pan and cover with lid for 2 minutes. Uncover and cook for 10 minutes.

Serve with tandur roti.

JUNGBARI PULAO

½ kg. meat
½ tbsp. ground garlic
½ tbsp. ground ginger
2 grated onions
Salt
1 cup beaten curds
Thick milk of 1 coconut

2 tbsp. ghee
1 large minced tomato
1 tsp. whole garam masala

Grind 10 red chillies, 12 cloves garlic, ½" piece ginger.

Boil the meat with ground ginger and garlic. Heat ghee, brown onions and garam masala. Cook till light brown, add ground spices and fry well. Put in meat and tomatoes. Add beaten curds. When boiling add thick coconut milk and salt. Cook till thick. Add boiled potatoes, if desired. Spread over coconut rice.

Coconut Rice: 2 cups rice, ½ tsp. turmeric, 1 tsp.

salt, thin milk of 1 coconut, ½ tsp. whole garam masala, 2 tbsp. ghee, 5-6 curry leaves, 1-2 cups water.

Fry curry leaves and spices in hot ghee, then add turmeric, salt and rice. Fry for a few minutes, then add coconut milk. Cook till dry; then add as much water as needed. Cover pan and put rice in a moderate oven to dry for about 15 minutes.

MASOOR PULAO

¼ kg. boiled mince
1 cup boiled whole masoor
2 cups boiled rice
½ kg. boiled and peeled small potatoes
1 large tomato, minced
4 minced onions
Salt
1 tsp. garam masala powder
¾ cups beaten curds

¼ bunch cut coriander
Some cut mint
6 whole green chillies
8 tbsp. ghee
2 sliced hard-boiled eggs

Grind 6 red chillies, 6 cloves garlic, 1 tsp. cummin, 2 tbsp. coriander seeds.

Heat half the ghee, fry onions till browned; put in ground spices and fry well. Add salt, green chillies, tomatoes and cook well for a few minutes. Add mince, masoor, curds, potatoes, mint, coriander leaves and garam masala powder. Arrange rice on top. Heat remaining ghee and pour over this, cover and cook for 15 minutes. Turn out into a plate, with rice underneath and mince on top. Decorate with sliced eggs.

PRAWN PATIA RICE RING

Patia

- 1 cup cleaned shelled prawns
- 2 cut onions
- 2 cut tomatoes
- 1 tbsp. coriander leaves
- Salt
- 4 peeled and cut drumsticks
- 2 tbsp. ghee
- 1 cup thick coconut milk
- Walnut-size lump of jaggery
- ½ cup tamarind water

Grind 5 green chillies, 4 red chillies, 6 cloves garlic ½ tsp. turmeric, ¾ tsp. cummin seeds, 1 tsp. garam masala powder.

Mix oil and ghee, and heat. Fry onions till golden brown; add ground spices and fry. Add tomatoes, coriander leaves, salt and jaggery and stir. Put in prawns, and stir well. Add coconut milk and drumsticks. Cover pan and cook on a slow fire till drumsticks are tender. Add tamarind water and cook till gravy is thick. Fill into rice ring.

Rice Ring

- 1 cup rice (boiled)
- 1 tbsp. ghee
- ½ tsp. cummin seeds
- 1 tbsp. chopped coriander leaves
- Salt

Heat ghee, fry cummin seeds and mix into boiled rice with salt and coriander leaves. Press firmly into a greased ring mould. Leave for 10 minutes. Unmould whilst warm.

CHEESE KOFTA CURRY

Koftas

¼ kg. mashed potatoes	Salt
1 tbsp. cornflour	¼ cup grated cheese
1 egg	Oil to fry
¼ tsp. chilli powder	

Mix all the ingredients well together (except oil). Form into medium-sized balls, and fry till golden brown in hot oil. Drain on paper in a colander.

Curry

1 kg. chopped tomatoes	2 medium-sized onions chopped
¼ kg. bones	Juice of ½ lemon
8 cups water	1 tbsp. white flour
2 tbsp. ghee	6 red chillies (broken into halves)
Salt	6 cloves garlic crushed
1½ tsp. sugar	10 curry leaves
small peeled and chopped beetroot	½ tsp. mustard seeds

Put tomatoes, salt, bones, water, onions and beetroot in a pan. Bring to boiling point, then simmer for half an hour. Remove when it reduces to a thick stock. Mix flour in it when cool.

Heat ghee and fry the remaining ingredients. Add the stock and cook uncovered for 10 minutes. Add sugar and lemon juice.

Serve with pea pulao.

PRAWN KORMA

2 cups shelled prawns
¼ kg. beaten curds
Salt
½ tsp. chilli powder
¼ tsp. turmeric
3 tbsp. oil
¾ tsp. garam masala
2 tbsp. cut coriander leaves

Grind 50 gm. cashewnuts, 25 gm. sesame seeds, 25 gm. poppy seeds, 6 green chillies, a handful of coriander leaves.

Mix prawns with curds, salt, chilli powder and turmeric and set aside for ½ an hour. Heat oil, and fry ground ingredients. Add prawns with curds and stir well. Simmer on a slow fire till prawns are done and the gravy becomes thick. Sprinkle garam masala and chopped coriander on top.

Serve with rice or parathas.

AAKHI MURGI

1¼ kg. chicken
¾ cup ghee
¼ kg. mince meat
Salt
3 medium onions finely chopped
1 cup curds

Grind 2 tbsp. coriander seeds, 4 red chillies, salt, 10 cloves garlic, ½" ginger.

Chop liver and giblets. Fry chopped onions and mince in 2 tbsp. ghee till brown. Add half the ground spices, liver and giblets and fry for 2-3 minutes. When cool, stuff into the chicken, and tie up.

Mix remaining ground spices in curds. Make a few cuts over chicken and rub curd mixture well over it. Heat remaining ghee and place the chicken in it. Seal pan with dough, cover tightly, and keep on a medium fire. Put few live charcoals on top of lid, or place in a medium oven (350°F) for ½ an hour. Unseal, turn chicken, and reseal pan. Cook for 20 more minutes. Open pan and fry chicken well till liquid in pan is dry.

Serve with parathas and onion-lemon salad.

SPINACH PRAWN SOUFFLE

¼ cup boiled prawns
Salt
3 eggs, separated
2 cut spring onions
2 chopped green chillies
4 tbsp. butter
4 tbsp. flour

1 cup milk
4 large bunches of cleaned spinach

Boil the finely chopped spinach with a pinch of soda. Mix spinach, prawns, onions, chillies and salt. Keep aside. Mix flour and milk till smooth. Heat butter, add flour mixture and stir till very thick and smooth. Add beaten egg yolks and spinach mixture. Fold in stiffly beaten egg whites. Pour into a creased dish and bake in a moderate oven (375°F) for ½ an hour.

Serve immediately.

MEAT IN BREAD LOAF

- ½ litre milk
- 3 tbsp. cornflour
- 2 chopped onions
- 1 large cut tomato
- ¼ tsp. chilli powder
- 2 chopped hard-boiled eggs
- 2 chopped capsicums
- Few chopped coriander leaves
- 2 stalks cut celery
- ¼ kg. boiled peas
- ½ kg. meat
- 1 loaf sandwich bread
- Ghee

Cut the meat into small cubes and boil it with salt. Remove top and centre of bread, leaving just the crust. Fry the crust in ½ cup ghee till brown. In 2 tbsp. ghee fry onions and capsicums for few minutes. Then add cornflour mixed with milk and cook till thick. Next add tomatoes, peas, meat, celery, salt and one egg. Mix well and fill into the bread. Garnish with the other egg, coriander leaves and chilli powder.

MURG AND MAKAI SOUFFLE

- 1 cup tinned or fresh boiled corn
- 4 eggs, separated
- 1 small flaked chicken
- ¼ cup stock
- 4 tbsp. flour
- 4 tbsp. margarine
- ½ cup grated cheese
- Salt
- Pepper
- Chilli powder to taste
- 2 cups milk

Melt margarine, put in flour and cook for 2 minutes. Remove from fire and add milk and stock. Return to heat and stir till thick. Add salt, pepper and chilli powder. Remove from fire, cool slightly and add yolks, corn, cheese and chicken. Fold in stiffly beaten whites and pour into a greased dish. Bake for half an hour in a moderately hot oven (400°F).

WALNUT MEAT LOAF

- ½ kg. mince
- 1 tsp. ginger
- 1 tsp. garlic
- 3 tbsp. tomato sauce
- 2 eggs
- Salt
- Pepper
- ¼ tsp. grated nutmeg
- ½ cup walnuts, finely chopped
- 2 small onions finely chopped
- 3 slices bread (soaked in milk)

Garnish: 1 cut lettuce, 1 sliced tomato, 1 sliced capsicum, 1 sliced hard-boiled egg, some sprigs of parsley.

Boil the mince with ginger and garlic; then grind it finely. Mix all the ingredients well together, pack firmly into a greased mould and bake at 350°F for ½ an hour. Remove from the mould and decorate with the garnish.

ANANAS SALAD

- 1 small tin diced pineapple
- 1 medium celery, chopped
- Salt
- ¼ cup grated cheese
- 2/3 cup well flavoured mayonnaise
- Few lettuce leaves
- ½ cup fresh pomegranate seeds
- ½ cup chopped walnuts
- 2 boiled peeled and cut potatoes

Mix all the ingredients except lettuce, walnuts and ¼ cup pomegranate seeds. Chill till ready for use. Mix in walnuts before serving, and decorate with lettuce leaves and pomegranate seeds. (Chopped peanuts may be substituted for walnuts.)

SPANISH CHICKEN RICE

2 cups rice
3 large sliced onions
Salt
1 cup peas
1 tsp. chilli powder
½ tsp. turmeric
1 sliced hard-boiled egg
Parsley

1 kg. chicken cut and boiled
3 cups stock
Ghee to fry

Sauce: ¼ kg. blanched tomatoes ground, 1 minced onion, 6 cloves thinly sliced garlic, ½" ginger thinly sliced, salt, 2 chopped green chillies, 1 tbsp. ghee.

For sauce, fry onion, ginger, garlic and green chillies for a few minutes; add salt and tomatoes. Boil for a few minutes. Keep aside.

Fry chicken pieces in ghee and keep aside when browned.

To prepare rice, fry onions in 3 tbsp. ghee till brown. Add rice, peas, salt, turmeric and chilli powder. Fry well, then add chicken stock. When water dries, put pan into oven for 10 minutes.

Spread the rice in dish, lay chicken pieces on sides and in centre and cover with sauce. Decorate with sliced egg and parsley.

KAJU TOFFEE

85 gm. butter
1 tbsp. golden syrup
1 tin condensed milk
½ cup chopped and warmed cashewnuts
1 cup sugar

Mix sugar and syrup. Melt butter and add to sugar; cook over low heat till sugar dissolves. Add condensed milk and stir. Cook for about 20 minutes till colour is golden, and mixture forms into a small ball when a little is dropped into some cold water. Add cashewnuts, remove from heat, allow bubbles to settle and pour into a greased tray. Cut into squares when cool, using a knife dipped in hot water and wiped dry.

ZARDA PULAO

½ kg. washed Delhi rice
1 cup sugar
4 gm. saffron, ground in 1 tsp. rose water
2 tbsp. raisins
Few blanched and cut almonds and pistachios
Juice of 2 lemons
¼ cup ghee
5 cloves
1 stick cinnamon
5 cardamoms
22 gm. whole turmeric

Melt the sugar in two cups of water. Tie the turmeric in muslin and boil it in 5 cups water; when the water is coloured, strain. Parboil rice in this water.

and sieve. Pour lemon juice over the rice, toss and mix, and rinse through with cold water. Put rice in sugar water.

Melt ghee separately in a small pan and fry the spices. Add to rice and sugar water, cover and cook on a slow fire, after stirring in the saffron, raisins and nuts. When the water dries, place in oven for 10 minutes, or seal edges of pan with a dough of flour and water and cook with a few coals on top and a slow fire below.

For Pineapple Zarda

Use small tin of pineapple, ¾ cup sugar and the pineapple syrup. Measure the syrup, and add sufficient water to make up 2 cups of liquid. The drained pineapple should be cut into small pieces, and mixed into rice along with nuts and raisins.

BAIDE-KA-HALWA

12 eggs, separated	6 cardamoms
1 cup ghee	Few sliced almonds and
1 cup sugar	silver foil

Beat whites into soft peaks. Fry cardamoms in ghee. Add sugar and 1 tbsp. water. Add yolks and whites and stir slowly. Lower heat and stir constantly till well blended and thick. Be careful to remove from fire before ghee begins to appear on surface. Spread in a large greased serving plate. Cover with silver foil, and sprinkle almonds on top.

RICE CAKE

½ cup butter
¼ tsp. grated lemon rind
1 cup castor sugar

4 eggs
250 gm. ground rice

Cream butter and lemon rind well; add sugar gradually, beating all the time. Add egg yolks one at a time, beating well after each addition. Beat whites stiff, and fold into mixture with the rice. Pour into a greased tin 8" wide and slightly deep. Bake at 375°F for one hour. Its rough texture is delicious.

FRUIT AND MAVA GHAS KA HALWA

1½ ltrs milk
1 cup sugar
15 gm. china grass
125 gm. dried milk (mava)
1 tsp. cardamom powder
½ tsp. cochineal

6 large, finely chopped chickoos
4 oranges, peeled and segmented
Few sliced almonds for garnishing

Boil milk and sugar together for 5 minutes, add china grass and cook till it dissolves; then add crumbled mava and stir till it melts. Remove from fire, add cochineal and cardamom powder. Pour into a shallow dish. Keep in a cool place, or on ice, till nearly set. Place in the fruit gently. When set firmly cut into diamond shapes. Sprinkle with almonds whilst serving.

SAFFRON PISTA CAKE

- ½ cup butter
- ½ cup sugar
- 2 large eggs
- 1|3 cup milk
- 2 cups flour
- 2 tsp. baking powder
- ¼ tsp. salt
- ½ tsp. saffron
- 2 tbsp. chopped pistas
- ¾ cup raisins

Sift the flour, baking powder and salt together. Cream butter, add sugar and beat till fluffy. Beat in eggs, one at a time. Roast the saffron and soak it in 2 tbsp. hot water. Add saffron water to egg mixture then add flour alternately with milk. Sift the nuts with a little flour to prevent sinking to bottom of cake. Add nuts to the cake mixture. Spread in a well greased pan, and bake at 350°F for one hour. Cool on rack for 10 minutes before removing from tin. This cake tastes better if served after 24 hours.

FREEZER STRAWBERRY ICE CREAM

- 1 basket strawberries (cleaned and crushed)
- ½ cup powdered sugar
- ½ cup sweet lime juice
- 1 tbsp. gelatine powder
- 400 gm. fresh cream
- 4 tbsp. milk
- 4 tbsp. sugar

Mix strawberries with sweet lime juice and ½ cup sugar; refrigerate for 3-4 hours. Chill cream, add 4 tbsp. sugar and milk and whip till thick. Fold in the strawberry pulp, and pour into ice trays. Stir mixture once whilst it freezes.

MANGO MOUSSE

1 cup mango pulp	1 tbsp. gelatine (soaked
4 tbsp. sugar	in ¼ cup cold water)
1 cup fresh cream	1 peeled and sliced mango

Mix mango pulp and sugar. Heat gelatine, add to mango and place over bowl of ice; stir frequently. When it begins to thicken, fold in whipped cream and pour into a wetted mould to set. When firm, unmould, and serve with mango slices arranged on top and sides.

CHICKOO SOUFFLE

1¼ cups chickoo pulp	1 tbsp. cornflour
6 eggs	½ tsp. vanilla essence
400 gm. fresh cream	3 envelopes gelatine (soaked
2 cups milk	in ½ cup cold water)
1¼ cups castor sugar	
3 peeled and sliced chickoos	

Beat yolks well, beat in 1 cup sugar and cornflour. Add milk and stir and cook till thick; remove from heat and add vanilla essence. Cool over pan of ice, stirring frequently. Heat gelatine, and add to custard, along with fruit pulp; chill well till it begins to set. Whip chilled cream. Beat whites till stiff; add ¼ cup sugar gradually, beating well after each addition of sugar. Fold in both cream and whites into custard lightly. Pour into a serving bowl and chill till set. Arrange sliced chickoos on top before serving.

SHEER KHURMA

- 2 litres milk, scalded and reduced to 1½ litres
- 1 cup sugar
- 2 tbsp. ghee
- ¼ cup seviyan, broken
- 3 tbsp. sultanas
- 2 tbsp. raisins
- 1 tbsp. sliced or pounded almonds
- 1 tbsp. sliced or pounded pistachios
- ½ tsp. nutmeg powder
- ½ tsp. cardamom powder
- ½ tsp. cardamom powder
- 2 tbsp. boiled and peeled charoli
- 6 coarsely chopped kharaks (dry dates)

Heat ghee, fry vermicelli, raisins and sultanas till brown. In the milk, add sugar and heat till it dissolves. Add the fried ingredients, and all the remaining ingredients. Simmer uncovered for 20 minutes. Serve in bowls or glasses.

This is a festive drink, and should be served warm.

KAJU CURD DELIGHT

- 1 tbsp. cornflour
- ½ kg. beaten curds
- 1 tin condensed milk
- ½ tsp. saffron (heated and powdered)
- 2 tbsp. hot water
- ¼ tsp. yellow food colouring
- 50 gm. finely cut or coarsely chopped cashewnuts

Mix cornflour to a smooth paste in ¼ cup water. Mix heated saffron powder and colouring in hot water.

Beat curds and mix with condensed milk and cook till it starts boiling. Remove from fire and add cornflour. Return to heat, stir and cook till thick. Mix in saffron. Pour into a bowl and chill. Sprinkle cashewnuts on top before serving.

KHARBUZ GULAB

1 melon	2 envelopes gelatine
1 tin condensed milk	3-4 tbsp. rose water
3 cups water	1 tsp. cardamom powder
1 tbsp. cornflour	Silver foil

Cut the melon in half, scoop out the centre and mash it. Cut wedges into shell and leave aside. Mix the cornflour in ½ cup water. Dissolve the gelatine in ½ cup cold water. Mix water and condensed milk and cook till boiling. Add cornflour and stir till thick. Remove from fire, add gelatine and cardamoms and stir over pan of ice till cool. Add rose water and melon. When cold, pour into the melon shells. When set, cover with silver foil.

SHAHI TUKRE

¼ kg. fresh cream	½ tsp. cardamom powder
1 ltr. milk	1 tbsp. rose water
1 cup sugar	1 sandwich bread (brown)
Few chopped almonds and pistachios	1 pink rose
	Silver foil

Cut the bread into thick slices and fry them brown. Boil the milk on a low fire till it reduces to ½ ltr. Add sugar and bring again to boiling point. Put in the fried bread and cook gently till it soaks most of the milk. Add rose water and cardamom powder. Lay bread in serving dish, and cover with cream. Sprinkle chopped nuts on top and also a few rose petals and silver foil.

MAVA BREAD BAKE

3 cups milk
125 gm. sugar
125 gm. dried milk (mava)
4 eggs.
1 small loaf bread

1 tsp. margarine
1 tsp. cardamom powder
½ tsp. saffron
Silver foil

Soak the mava in some cold milk. Slice the bread, and soak it in water. Squeeze out water from bread. Heat milk with sugar, add mava and stir till it dissolves. Put in bread, saffron and cardamom. Cook for a little while till slightly thick. Add margarine and remove from fire. When slightly cool, beat in the eggs. Bake in a greased dish, in a moderate oven (325°F) for half an hour. Serve hot or cold, with silver foil on top

DOODHI-KA-HALWA

2¼ kg. grated white
   pumpkin
250 gm. dried milk (mava)
125 gm. sugar
175 gm. ghee

2 tbsp. rose water
½ tsp. cardamom powder
Green colouring
Few sliced almonds

Boil the pumpkin till it reduces to ½ kg. Heat ghee, fry the pumpkin well in it, then add sugar and cook well till quite dry. Then add mava and cardamom powder. Fry well till the mava dissolves. Add colouring and rose water. Put into a serving dish and sprinkle almonds on top.

ROAT

- ¼ kg. semolina
- ¼ kg. powdered sugar
- ¼ kg. ghee
- 5 eggs
- 1 tsp. mixed cardamom and nutmeg powder
- Few sliced almonds
- ¼ tsp. saffron
- ¼ tsp. orange food colouring
- ½ tbsp. milk
- 1 tbsp. poppy seeds

Heat and powder the saffron and mix it with colouring and milk. Beat ghee in a bowl till very soft; add sugar and beat again. Add eggs alternately with the semolina, beating well after each addition. Add cardamom and nutmeg powder and saffron mixture. Pour into a greased dish, sprinkle almonds and poppy seeds on top, and let it stand for 20 minutes. Then bake at 350°F for 45 minutes, or till done.

CARAMEL PHIRNI

2 ltrs. milk
¾ cup sugar
3 tbsp cornflour
1 tbsp. rose water
125 gm. dried milk (mava)
3 tbsp. sugar

Few sliced almonds and pistachios
Silver foil

Boil the milk on a low heat till it reduces to 1 lit. Add ¾ cup sugar. Burn 3 tbsp. sugar and add to milk. When dissolved, add mashed mava. Mix cornflour and ¼ cup water to a smooth paste, add in and stir till smooth and thick. Remove from heat, add rose water, and pour into a dish. Chill. Cover with silver foil and sliced nuts.

KHOPRA PAAK

1 grated coconut
125 gm. sugar
50 gm. dried milk (mava)
¼ tsp. cochineal

2 tbsp. kewra or rose water
4 tbsp water

Mix coconut, sugar and water and cook on a medium fire till the sugar dissolves. Stir in crumbled mava, and stir well till dry. Add colouring and flavouring off the fire. Spread on a greased tray and pat down with a greased knife or spatula. Cut into squares when cold. Arrange in a plate and cover with silver foil.

MAH KHUDI

1 ltr. milk
125 gm. dried milk (mava)
125 gm. sugar
2 tbsp. rose water
¼ tsp. orange food colouring

60 gm. nishasta
1 tsp. cardamom powder

Dissolve mava in some cold milk. Dissolve colouring and nishasta in ¼ cup water. Heat the milk, sugar and mava and cook well till it dissolves. Then add colouring and nishasta. Cook and stir well till thick. Remove from fire, add rose water. Pour into a dish to set. Sprinkle cardamom powder on top.

DOODHI-KI-MITHAS

1½ kg. grated white pumpkin
1 tin condensed milk
2 tbsp. rose water
3 cups water
1 tsp. cardamom powder

2 tbsp. cornflour
3 tbsp. sugar, if necessary
Few sliced almonds

Put condensed milk and water in a pan, add pumpkin and cook slowly for 15-20 minutes. Add cornflour mixed in ½ cup water, and stir till thick. Remove from fire. Add rose water, cardamom powder and the sugar if needed. Chill well. Garnish with almonds.

KELE-KI-KHEER

6 ripe, green bananas, mashed
Thick milk of 1 coconut
4 tbsp. sugar
3 tbsp. ghee
2 tbsp. wheat flour
½ tsp. cardamom powder
½ tsp. nutmeg powder

Heat ghee and fry the wheat flour till lightly browned. Add coconut milk gradually, stirring all the time. When smooth add the bananas and sugar and cook till slightly thick. Sprinkle cardamom and nutmeg powders, then remove from fire and serve whilst still warm.

SWEET COCONUT CROQUETTES

½ fresh coconut grated
1 tbsp. poppy seeds
4 tbsp. sugar
25 gm. raisins
1 tsp. cardamom powder
½ tsp. grated nutmeg
12-15 slices bread
Ghee for frying

To make filling, heat 2 tbsp. ghee and fry the coconut till brownish red. Add sugar, poppy seeds and raisins and fry till sugar melts. Take off the fire. Add cardamom and nutmeg.

Soak bread slices in salted water for ½ minute, and press water out by squeezing between palms. Fill with coconut mixture, fold over and seal up edges and fry in hot ghee till browned well on both sides. Drain and serve at once whilst hot.

SHAHI FIRNI

½ ltr. milk
200 gm. dried milk (mava)
½ to ¾ cups sugar
2 tbsp. rose water
¼ tsp. saffron (heated and powdered)
30 gm. wheat germ (nishasta)

1 tbsp. rice flour
¼ tsp. cardamom powder
Few rose petals
Silver foil

Mix the nishasta and rice flour separately in cold water. Separately mix mava to a paste with some hot milk; add to milk and stir well. Add rice flour and cook for a few minutes; then add nishasta and cook till thick, stirring all the time. Add saffron, remove from the fire and add rose water. Pour into a dish and chill. Sprinkle cardamom powder on top and decorate with silver foil and rose petals.

GUAVA CUSTARD

2 cups milk
2 tbsp. custard powder
4 tbsp. sugar
¼ tsp. vanilla essence

2 cups peeled cut guavas (seeds removed)

Mix milk, sugar and custard powder till smooth: place on heat, and stir till boiling. Add the guavas, and cook for 5 minutes on a fast fire till guavas are soft, and custard thick. Remove from fire and mix in the essence. Pour into a bowl and chill before serving.

MAVA KESAR HALWA

- 1 ltr. milk
- 250 gm. dried milk (mava)
- 10 gm. china grass
- ½ tsp. ground saffron
- ¼ tsp. cardamom powder
- ½-¾ cup sugar according to taste
- Few sliced almonds for garnishing

Boil china grass in 1 cup water till dissolved. Heat milk, mava and sugar together; simmer for 10 minutes, add the china grass and cook for 5 minutes. Stir in the saffron and cardamom and remove from heat when it boils once. Pour into a shallow dish to set. Cut into squares and serve with a few sliced almonds sprinkled on top.

MANGO CREME

- Juice or pulp of 4 mangoes
- 5 tbsp. sugar
- 2 cups milk
- 2 tbsp. custard powder
- Chopped walnuts
- 2 peeled and sliced mangoes
- 250 gm. fresh cream
- ¼ kg. square or oblong sponge cake

Remove centre of cake, leaving 1 inch all round the sides and at the base. Mix milk, 4 tbsp. sugar, custard powder and mango pulp together in a pan, cook and stir till thick and boiling, then cool. Pour into centre of cake. Beat cream with 1 tbsp. sugar and spread over the mango pulp. Decorate with walnuts and mango slices.

CARAMEL SOUFFLE

- 1½ tbsp. cornflour
- 3 cups milk
- ¼ cup brown sugar
- ¼ cup castor sugar
- 2 tbsp. margarine
- 3 eggs
- Vanilla essence
- 1½ tbsp. gelatine powder
- Some powdered biscuits for the top

Mix the gelatine in 4 tbsp. water. Melt fat, add brown sugar and cook till it melts. Keep aside. Mix cornflour and egg yolks; add milk and mix to a smooth paste. Pour into brown sugar, cook till dissolved and thick. Place over a pan of ice, add gelatine and stir well. Beat whites very stiff, put in the castor sugar gradually, add vanilla and fold into souffle. Chill till set. Sprinkle powdered biscuits on top.

CHOCO-NUT CUSTARD

- 3 cups milk
- 3 eggs
- ½ cup coarsely pounded walnuts
- ¼ tsp. almond essence
- 2 tbsp. cocoa powder
- 6 tbsp. sugar

Mix cocoa with some warm milk till smooth. Stir into the remaining milk till well blended. Whisk eggs and sugar in a bowl till thick; add to milk and mix well. Then add essence and nuts. Pour into a shallow baking dish, and bake in a medium oven for ½-¾ hour, or till set. Serve hot or cold. May be served with plain custard or whipped cream if so desired.

CHOC SEMOLINA WHIP

½ ltr. milk
1 cup fresh cream
4 tbsp. sugar
Vanilla
2 tbsp. cocoa powder

4 tbsp. semolina
1 bar coarsely chopped chocolate
Few chopped cherries

Add 1 tbsp. sugar to the cream and beat it till thick. Mix cocoa in some hot milk, pour into remaining milk, add sugar. Then sprinkle the semolina, a teaspoonful at a time, and stir well. Cook till thick. Remove from the fire, add a few drops of vanilla. When cool, whisk well, add the cream and whisk again. Pour into a bowl. When set, sprinkle chocolate and cherries on top.

GOOSEBERRY MOULD

½ kg. gooseberries (to be hulled and cleaned)
½ cup water
2 tbsp. cornflour

Sugar to taste (bet. ½ to ¾ cup)
Little castor sugar
½ cup cream

Put the gooseberries (or any well flavoured fruit) in a saucepan with the water and stew til' the fruit softens to a pulp. Drain off the juice through a fine sieve. Mix cornflour with cold water to form a smooth paste, then add it to the fruit juice and cook it for 2-3 minutes. Push the fruit through a sieve and stir it into the hot mixture. Sweeten to taste and cool. Then pour into individual bowls or a large bowl. Sprinkle the top with a little castor sugar and chill. Serve, decorated with whipped cream.

This can also be used as filling for a flan.

STRAWBERRY SOUFFLE

¼ kg. cream
6 eggs
¼ kg. sugar
2 cups mashed strawberries

¼ tsp. cochineal
3 tbsp. gelatine

Garnish: few whole strawberries. Some cornflakes or crushed plain biscuits (Marie).

Dissolve the gelatine in hot water. Whisk yolks and sugar till thick and add cooled gelatine. Fold in cream, well whisked egg whites, strawberry pulp and cochineal. Stir well and set in a glass dish. Decorate with whole strawberries and cornflakes or crushed biscuits.

PINEAPPLE SOUFFLE

6 eggs
¼ kg. cream
1 tbsp. castor sugar
1 tbsp. cornflour
1 tin pineapple cubes
1½ cups milk

5 tsp. gelatine
¼ cup sugar
¼ cup pineapple syrup

Mix yolks, sugar and cornflour. Add milk and cook till thick. Place on a pan of ice. Soak gelatine in syrup and add to milk, stirring all the time. Beat cream with castor sugar and fold into pudding. Add pineapple cubes. Whip up whites and fold in. Pour into a dish and let it set. Decorate with cherries and pineapple cubes.

BANANA CLOUD

2 cups mashed bananas
2 tbsp. lemon juice
1 tsp. grated lemon rind
2 envelopes gelatine
¼ cup water
¼ cup sugar
1 pinch salt

4 egg whites
200 gm. fresh cream
2 tbsp. sugar
1 sliced banana
Few sliced cherries

Soak the gelatine in water. Whip the cream till thick with 2 tbsp. sugar. Mix banana, lemon juice, rind, 3 tbsp. sugar and salt well together. Heat gelatine and stir till dissolved, add to bananas and mix well. Leave to cool. Beat whites stiff, add remaining sugar and beat well. Fold into banana mixture. Fold in the cream. Chill until firm. Decorate with banana and cherry slices and serve.

STRAWBERRY CREAM TART

Pastry
150 gm. sifted flour
75 gm. margarine
1 egg yolk
2 tbsp. sugar
Cold water to mix

Filling
2 cups mashed strawberries
¼ cup sugar
Juice of ½ lemon
1 cup water
1½ tsp. cornflour

Garnish ¼ kg. sweetened whipped cream, 4 halved strawberries, 3 crushed plain biscuits (Marie).

Make pastry by mixing flour and margarine in a bowl till it resembles fine bread crumbs. Add yolk and sugar, then bind to a smooth dough with little cold water. Roll out ¼ inch thick, line a greased dish or tin with pastry, prick with fork and bake in a moderate oven (350°F) for 20 minutes.

Make filling by putting all ingredients in saucepan and cooking till thick. Cool. Fill into cooked pie shell. Pour cream on top and sprinkle powdered biscuit. Place halved strawberries on top. Keep cool till used.

CHOCOLATE PEAR TRIFLE

1 small sponge cake
1 tin pears
½ ltr. milk
¼ cup sugar
2 tbsp. cocoa powder
3 tbsp. cornflour

Few walnuts and cherries
1 cup fresh cream
Mock cream (see below)

Cut cake in slices and line a dish, pour pear syrup from can over it, then arrange pear slices. Mix the cocoa in 3 tbsp. hot water and add to cold milk. Add sugar and cornflour and stir well. Cook till thick. Cool. Stir in the cream. Pour over the pear slices. Chill well. Decorate with mock cream, walnuts, cherries.

MOCK CREAM

3 tbsp. margarine
6-8 tbsp. sieved icing sugar
1 tbsp. milk

2-3 drops vanilla essence

Beat the margarine well and add enough sugar to form a stiff consistency. Add vanilla and milk. Chill till used.

LEMON FLUFF

4 eggs
1 cup fine sugar
1 envelope gelatine
2|3 cup water
1|3 cup lemon juice
½ tsp. cream of tartar
1 tbsp. grated lemon rind
¼ kg. fresh cream
Cornflakes and cherries for top

In a saucepan, blend yolks, ½ cup sugar, gelatine, water and lemon juice. Cook over slow fire, stirring all the time till the mixture just boils. Stir in lemon rind. Place pan over bowl of ice, stirring occasonally till thick. Beat whites and cream of tartar till stiff, adding the rest of the sugar gradually. Fold in the lemon mixture and chill till set. Whip the cream with 3 tbsp. sugar till thick. Pour over the pudding. Sprinkle cornflakes and cherries on top.

PINEAPPLE DELIGHT

1 small tin pineapple (cubes)
2 pkts lemon jelly or any yellow jelly
1 small family pack vanilla ice cream
Few cut cherries

Dissolve the jelly in 2½ cups water and the tinned pineapple syrup. Cool over ice till nearly set. Beat in ice cream gradually and add most of the pineapple, saving a few bits for decoration. Pour into serving dish and decorate with cherries and pineapple pieces and chill.

MALPURAS

1 cup flour
1 egg
¼ tsp. saffron powdered
½ cup milk
½ cup water
½ cup sugar
Ghee or margarine to fry

Sift flour into a bowl, break in egg and stir well. Add some of the liquid and stir to smooth consistency. Add rest of the liquid and mix well. Stir in sugar and saffron and keep the bowl, covered, in a warm place for twelve hours.

Heat 2 tsp. ghee in frying pan, add enough mixture to make a medium sized pancake (approx. a ladle-full) and fry on both sides till golden brown. Serve warm with clotted cream (malai).

EQUIVALENT MEASURES AND WEIGHTS

Pinch, dash	= less than $\frac{1}{8}$ teaspoon
3 teaspoons	= 1 tablespoon
2 tablespoons	= 1 oz. liquid or fat
4 tablespoons	= $\frac{1}{4}$ cup
16 tablespoons	= 1 cup or 8 oz.
$\frac{1}{4}$ cup = $\frac{1}{8}$ pint	= $\frac{1}{2}$ gill
$\frac{1}{2}$ cup = $\frac{1}{4}$ pint	= 1 gill
1 cup = $\frac{1}{2}$ pint	= 2 gills

METRIC EQUIVALENTS

Weight

$$1 \text{ oz.} = 28\frac{1}{2} \text{ grams (roughly 30 gm.)}$$
$$3\frac{1}{2} \text{ oz.} = 100 \text{ grams}$$
$$1 \text{ lb. } 1\frac{1}{2} \text{ oz.} = \frac{1}{2} \text{ kilogram} = 500 \text{ grams}$$
$$2 \text{ lb. } 3 \text{ oz.} = 1 \text{ kilogram}$$

Liquid

1 litre = 35 oz. = $1\frac{3}{4}$ pint.

Dry

1 rounded teaspoon	= 5 grams
1 rounded tablespoon	= 14 grams = $\frac{1}{2}$ oz.
2 rounded tablespoons	= 29 grams = 1 oz.
1 well rounded tablespoon	= 22 grams = $\frac{3}{4}$ oz.

OVEN TEMPERATURES AND REGULO NUMBERS

Description	Temperature in °F	Gas. No.
Very slow or cool	under 250	$\frac{1}{4}$ to $\frac{1}{2}$
Slow	250-300	$\frac{1}{2}$ to 1
Very Moderate or Moderately Slow	300-325	1 to 2
Moderate	325-360	3 to 5
Moderately hot	375-400	6 to 7
Hot	425-450	8 to 9
Very hot	450-500	9

ON FRYING WELL

Deep-fried foods, such as cutlets, kababs, vadas and samosas, should be drained in a sieve or colander which has been doubly lined with brown paper. This prevents sogginess and excessive greasiness When heating the oil, squeeze in a few drops of lemon juice so that the oil odour evaporates.

Deep frying should be done in a thick, deep pan (karhai); medium frying in a frying pan, and shallow frying on a griddle (tawa).

ON FRYING GROUND SPICES (MASALAS)

Heat oil well add ground spices (masala) and fry for 2-3 minutes. Then reduce heat, and continue to fry, stirring frequently. If it tends to stick to pan. add 1 tbsp. stock or water on the part which has stuck and scrape the pan quickly before it burns. Continue to fry in this way, till the ghee or oil surfaces in bubbles to the top.

TO PREVENT LUMPS

Custards, sauces and soups will never turn lumpy if the thickening agent (e.g., flour, arrowroot, custard powder or cornflour) is mixed in cold milk or water (or any other liquid) and added to the heated contents of a pan, off the fire. Then stir briskly and return to the fire. Continue to stir till it reaches the desired consistency.

FOR EASY GRINDING

Chillies

Red chillies should be soaked overnight (or 2-3 hours in hot water) to make them soft. If the receipe requires that masala should be ground in vinegar, soak chillies in vinegar 2-3 hours before grinding.

Coconut

Fresh coconut should be grated and then ground; similarly, dry coconut should be grated and then ground.

Coriander, Cummin Seeds, Garam Masalas, Aniseed, etc.

Should be heated for a few minutes either on a griddle (tawa) or in an oven. When cool, they become crisp, and hence easy to grind.

Cashewnuts, Peanuts, etc.

These should be peeled, and coarsely pounded before grinding.

GRATED ONIONS

Peel onions and grate on a large grater. The part which cannot be grated should be ground. Put the grated onion in a muslin or thin cloth and squeeze out the juice. Fry the strained onion in ghee or oil as instructed in the recipe, adding the juice later, after the onion or masala is browned.

TO SKIN TOMATOES

Bring water to boiling point; put in the tomatoes, cover with lid and remove at once from the fire. Keep covered for 10 minutes. Drain off the water. Remove skin when slightly cool; then grind or sieve the tomatoes.

ON BOILING SPAGHETTI

Boil water with ½ tsp. salt and 1-2 tbsp. oil (depending on quantity of water used). Put in spaghetti or macaroni, and cook on a brisk fire (without lid) till done. Drain in a colander, and hold under a tap of cold water for a few seconds till all the starch is drained away. If boiled spaghetti is to be kept overnight, put into a bowl of chilled water and keep in the refrigerator till required.

MASHED POTATOES

Heat water with ½ tsp. salt till it reaches boiling point. Add peeled and cut potatoes. Cook uncovered till soft. Drain, and mash immediately whilst hot. Add salt and pepper to taste.

For Creamed Potatoes

Prepare the same way as for mashed potatoes, adding milk and butter along with the salt and pepper. (For ¼ kg. potatoes use ½ cup milk and 1 tbsp. butter.)

BIRISTA (BROWNED ONIONS)

A good birista is essential for almost ninety per cent of Moghlai dishes. It is a rather tricky thing to do, but one attains perfection with practice.

Heat ghee or oil in a deep pan (karhai). Add finely sliced onions, and stir frequently on a brisk fire till they are golden brown (be careful not to brown them too much or food will have a bitter flavour). Remove at once and spread over brown paper. Leave for 5 minutes and crush whilst still warm, but crisp.

GARAM MASALA

This is used in numerous dishes, and consists of four spices: cinnamon, cloves, cardamoms and peppercorns

Heat 1 tbsp. peppercorns, ¾ tbsp. cloves, 1 tbsp. peeled cardamoms, and 8 two-inch sticks of cinnamon on a griddle for 2 minutes. Pound together when cool. Bottle and store till needed.

TO MAKE A GOOD JALI (LACE)

To make a good *jali* for cutlets and fried chicken, the eggs should be beaten with an egg whisk (but not till frothy). Add 1 tbsp. cold water for each egg. Dip the cutlets or chicken into egg, put into hot ghee, and make the *jali* by sprinkling the egg quickly on and around cutlets and reducing the heat. Cook on a slow fire till *jali* is crisp and brown.

COCONUT MILK

The best way to extract coconut milk is to grate a fresh coconut, grind it coarsely, and add as much hot water as is required (according to whether you need thick or thin milk). Leave for 5 minutes. Squeeze well, and strain the milk into a bowl.

To Prevent Curdling

Before adding coconut milk to a gravy or masala reduce the heat. Add milk and stir till it boils gently. After a few minutes, it can be allowed to boil fast, for it will not curdle.

TO PREVENT CURDLING OF CURDS

To prevent curds from curdling in a curry, always beat curds well till smooth, using an egg whisk. Reduce heat and add the curds. Stir well, then increase the heat. Keep stirring for 5 minutes, then let it cook as required in recipe. If curds are to be mixed with water before adding to a curry, add a teaspoon or tablespoon (depending on quantity) of channa flour (besan) or wheat flour to the curds and beat till smooth.

TO BOIL FISH

To boil fish so that it does not smell, wash it well, and put it in a shallow pan with a large sprig of mint, some salt, the juice of $\frac{1}{2}$-1 lemon and a few peppercorns. Simmer uncovered for a few minutes till fish is cooked.

A dash of lemon or vinegar when poaching fish also keeps it firm and prevents it from breaking.

TO TENDERISE MEAT

Tough meat which will not soften, in spite of applying ginger and garlic paste and prolonged boiling, can be tenderised in any one of the ways given below. For 1 kg. meat:—
1) Take $\frac{1}{2}$ a small raw papaaya, grind it with the skin, and add to meat.
2) Add 2 whole betel nuts (supari) to the meat.

3) Caramelise 1 tbsp. sugar and add; but when caramel is added, meat should be cooked on a slow fire.

GELATINE

Measure

In cold weather 14 gm. (½ oz.), 4 level teaspoons or one slightly rounded tablespoon is sufficient to set a pint (2 cups) of liquid.

In hot weather 21 gm. (¾ oz.) or one well-rounded tablespoon is needed to set a pint of liquid.

For a tall or large mould allow no more than 1¾ cups of liquid per 14 gm.

How to use

Soften the gelatine in cold water or juice. Dissolve this on gentle heat or, better still, place bowl in a basin of hot water on the stove. Stir with metal spoon and make certain that the gelatine is completely dissolved.

Do not boil gelatine as this will spoil flavour and reduce setting power. Add gelatine to the liquid, puree or cream, as the case may be, while warm. To cool the mixture stand the bowl in a colander with ice cubes round it.

The gelatine mixture must be poured into a mould when cold and about to set.

HOW TO CHOOSE VEGETABLES

Choose firm, tender and fresh looking vegetables. Avoid those with discoloration, blemishes, wrinkles and even the slightest rot. French beans must be flat, tender and an attractive green—not grey and hard and stringy. Cauliflowers should be compact and white; avoid the creamy ones with sprigs spreading and leaves yellowing. Cucumbers and cabbages should be firm and green. Tomatoes, cucumbers, capsicums and brinjals should have taut, shining skins; do not touch the soft ones. Discoloured or wilting lettuce or spinach should be left well alone. Potatoes, beetroots and carrots should be free from blemishes. Peas should be green and full, not flat or light coloured.

"PRETTY" COOL

Cut tender celery stalks into pieces, fringe ends and let them curl up and crispen in cold water. Do not throw away outer stalks and leaves; use them for stocks and soups.

Radishes bloom into flowers if cut down but not right through into sections and placed in ice water.

A vegetable aspic means a lot of work. Why not add to a pint of well-seasoned and strained tomato pulp, some gelatine melted in lemon juice, and chill into a salad ring. Fill it up with anything, boiled cauliflower sprigs in white sauce or masala prawns.

Talking of tomatoes, they lend themselves to all

shapes and fillings. You can have tomato pyramids with cheesy fillings between slices; or tomato baskets; or tomato segments filled with russian salad, like an accordion.

Chilled cucumber and carrots, peeled and scrubbed, make pretty garnishes. Cut out lengthwise strips from the outer circumference at regular intervals. Then slice them to get flowery shapes.

DELICIOUSLY RAW

Raw vegetables are fun to eat and full of flavour and vitamins. Slice cucumber thinly and marinate in salt and pepper. They are more digestible if the skin is left on.

Tomato wedges, peeled or unpeeled, can be sprinkled with salt and pepper and a touch of castor sugar.

Capsicums are easier to digest if blanched for a few seconds in salted, hot water. Remove stalk and seeds, and cut off bottom lobes. They will now slice easily into decorative rings.

Fresh, tender carrots and cabbages finely shredded are tasty and add substance to any salad.

Or, add well seasoned corn if you like.

Take half a grapefruit and toothpicks, invert grapefruit and insert sticks in and make a colourful porcupine with bits of vegetable, fruit and cheese on each toothpick.

CRISP AND TASTY

Do not leave a bunch of lettuce leaves soaking in water. Wash thoroughly in cold water; a little salt will help to loosen grit. Dry well in basket or wipe with cloth and leave in a cool, dry place till required.

Lettuce leaves can be served whole, cut up or shredded. However, perk them up with raw vegetables and different flavours. Add chopped parsley, sprigs of mint, bits of celery or a sprinkling of finely sliced onion. These flavours go well with chopped nuts, cheese and fruits.

Just before serving, spoon over french dressing or mayonnaise and toss.

THE SECRET OF PUFFY EGG WHITES

The first step is to have the bowl and beaters clean and dry. The best volume is achieved with a balloon whisk and an unlined copper bowl. A rotary beater or an electric one may be used also.

The egg whites should be at room temperature. They should be absolutely free from egg yolk, butter or any grease. Flavour with a pinch of salt, and add either few drops of lemon or 1/7 teaspoon cream of tartar to every four egg whites. These will help the whites to keep their volume and texture.

Beat the whites until they stand in stiff peaks but are still shiny, not dry and lifeless.

Before folding in, stir two or three tablespoons of the whites into the basic mixture. This facilitates the folding action. Do not stir. Work gently and do not overblend.

ECONOMY DRIVE

The pressure cooker is a boon and a must for the modern housewife. It saves on time and fuel and keeps the cooking area cooler. There is no watching and stirring. Since less water is used, nutrients are preserved. Less expensive foods are cooked deliciously; and so it is no chore to make dhal, soup or mashed potatoes and even tenderize tough meat.

Never discard meat and poultry bones. Use them to make soups and stocks. Pitch in tops and leaves of vegetables and the liquid from canned vegetables.

Liquids from canned fruits can be used to make fruit punches and gelatine desserts. This will save on sugar also.

Left-over bread goes straight to make dry crumbs. If you have a refrigerator then store it in a plastic bag for future use.

If you chill soup or stock, a thick layer of fat forms on top. Use this as a cooking medium.

SOUFFLE HINTS

Measure all the ingredients and assemble together the bowls, whisks and spoons. Have ice and the refrigerator handy for a cold souffle and the oven ready for a hot one.

Eggs beat up best at room temperature. They may be separated when cold, one by one and into clean bowls.

A little starch in the form of cornflour is essential to act as a thickening agent for the yolk mixture.

Yolks should be beaten thick and lemon coloured, pouring down in a ribbon.

The basic sauce or puree must be smooth and rich in flavour. The consistency and flavour of the souffle depends on this.

The air trapped in by the whisking is retained by (a) the correct use of gelatine and (b) by freezing in a cold souffle; and in a hot souffle by (a) the firm yolk base, (b) the stiffly beaten whites and (c) a hot oven. Most important, work deftly with a light action and do not overmix or over-beat.

Egg whites play an important part. In a cold souffle they impart the final volume and lightness whereas in the hot souffle they raise the mixture to nearly double its volume. Whites should be stiff yet moist, not dry.

It is also important to have the cream, sauce and whites of a more or less similar consistency. This enables them to mix smoothly.

GLOSSARY

Badam - almonds
Saunf - aniseed
Heeng - asaphoetida
Kababcheeni - allspice
Tej patta - bay leaf
Birista - browned fried onion
Shahjeera - caraway
Kaju - cashewnut
Mirchi - chillies
Charoli - chironjia sapida
Taj or *dalchini* - cinnamon
Lavang - cloves
Kothmir - coriander leaf
Dhania - coriander seed
Zeera - cummin seed
Kala draksha kismis - currants
Soova bhaji - dil leaves
Lal mirchi - dried chilli
Kopra - dried coconut
Sunth - dried ginger
Viryali - fennel
Methi dana - fenugreek seeds
Pawwa - flaked rice
Atta - flour
Nariel - fresh coconut
Lasan - garlic

Adrak - ginger
Besan - gramflour
Hari mirchi - green chillies
Gur - jaggery
Dal - lentils, pulses
Javantri - mace
Kokum - mangosteen
Bajri - millet
Poodina - mint
Rai - mustard
Jaiphal - nutmeg
Ajwan - parsley seed
Miri - peppercorns
Pista - pistachio
Khus khus - poppy seeds
Kismis - raisin
Jaffran, kesar - saffron
Sabudana - sago
Til - sesame seeds
Sozi/rava - semolina
Manuka - sultana
Sakarkand - sweet potato
Imli - tamarind
Haldi - turmeric
Seviya - vermicelli
Surka - vinegar
Maida - white flour
Doodhi - white pumpkin

JAICO BOOKS
bring to you
world famous classics
—the great works of literature
which you have always wanted
to read. Handsomely turned out
in handy size
and handsomely printed, set in
an especially clear, easy-read type,
JAICO BOOKS provide
the best in reading values,
at a price within
the reach of all.